# Introduction

A close friend gives me, his homosexual friend, money to help sponsor a poetry event. A few days later that same friend updates his Facebook status to say, "WHEN DID FAGGOTS START ROAMING THE EARTH SO FREELY? SMH, I FEEL ANOTHER HOLOCAUST COMING...LOL."

After seeing that post, I decided to monitor his page. I soon found out that this person I've known since middle school, I really didn't know at all. Like so many on various social networking websites, there's a great chance that he was pretending to be someone other than the person that he is when logged off. It made me wonder: Is the thirteen year old boy that wrote me on YouTube and told me that he hopes my girlfriend and I catch a bullet to the back of our heads going to find me or someone like myself and enforce his rage? Is the girl who wrote me on Facebook and told me that she would get killed for being openly gay in her town exaggerating or sending one of her last messages before hate and misunderstanding brings her life to an end? We can never be sure because the environment of social networking rarely provides us with the opportunity to know.

Still, the fact remains that the Internet is a roaring inspiration and one of the most powerful inspirations behind everything real today. How does this generation survive? How does this generation converse, break up, display love and find things out about one another? The World-Wide-Web. Right now you are about to mentally and emotionally log into some of your favorite websites (Facebook, Twitter and Youtube) and see how other people feel about religion, hate, suicide, "coming out," love, death, freedom and all things surrounding homosexuality by simply turning a page.

## Dedication

To my Nephew, Choose what your heart leads you to choose and understand everything, even the things you can never see yourself being.

This book is not in partnership with or sponsored by
FACEBOOK, TWITTER, OR YOUTUBE

**Out of The Closet**, Homosexuality, Homophobia, and everything In-Between,
**ONLINE**

## New message

**To** | Enter a friend's name or email address

**Message**

CHAPTER1
I've seen lots of normal things and few strange things in closets, I've seen big things and I've seen small things in closets, I've never seen a homosexual, or a human being struggling with sexual preference issues hiding in one. To assume that one is hiding something because they do not speak about it or to assume that one is hiding something out of shame because they have not told you or other people about it, is ignorant. We are born to love, we are not born with an obligation to love and tell others about the people or the way we choose to love. Imagine the confusion in trying to satisfy one half of the world by "coming out" and the other half by staying in, it's unnecessarily painful. Some things you shouldn't worry about and the sexual preference of others is one of those things.

**Send**   Cancel

**lawrence king i will remember**

cartermayes   12 videos   Subscribe

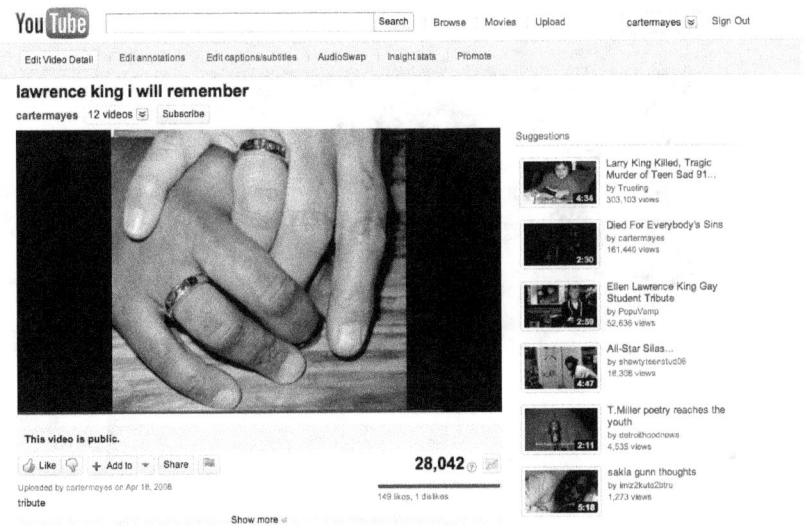

This video is public.

Like   + Add to   Share

Uploaded by cartermayes on Apr 18, 2008
tribute

28,042

149 likes, 1 dislikes

Show more

fundamentalist26 is already in hell, to follow, are all the other ignorant sociopaths on this page. They lack respect for human life, because they are brainwashed haters. mafiasdaughter 2 years ago 12

they neva sad he was hit n on him hey jus asked sumbody 2 b there valentine he culd of jus simply said no and kept it movin do u really think that sumbody shuld kill sum 1 jus bcuz they asked sumbody 2 b there valentine ????? if u think he deserved that u can go straight 2 hell bitch bajaburstqueen 2 years ago 20

u should go striaight 2 hell u if u think sumbody shuld die bcuz of there sexual orientation bajaburstqueen 2 years ago 21

your fucking ignorant, you dont understand shit so shut the fuck up and learn, cuz theres a lot of people who want to remember. studies have proved that most antigays actually are gay or bi hencoleman 2 years ago 8

all those who mocks gay is wrong ask ur self does god ask you to hate, i have many gay friend and i dnt give a crap what they do. i know they're human being gay is not a choice is how you born. its said if u have an extra y chromosome to male/female. so why hate? its just make you look ugly make you look like a monser who hate those who r brave comming out. gay/bi r every lonely unlike you str8 they have to hide their feeling toward those they love.so plz dnt h8...ok? xxAER0xx 2 years ago

3

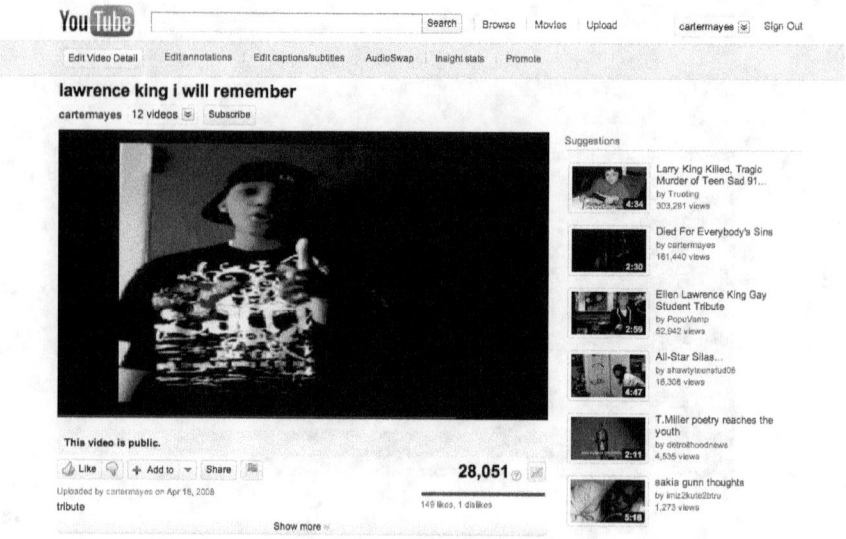

you know what i think we are in a world where we as human being are being discriminated against because of our race,what we do,what music we listen to and our sexuality i know this because i get it.I am a straight 15 year old boy and we should'nt judge people like(svlirio2001,AmericaHatesF aggots and fuckallthefaggots) for example.You are the one's who should burn in hell karma does'nt play and all you people like those users i mentioned you will get your share of discrimination some day misile005 2 years ago

What the fuck is wrong with you? Seriously the kid is dead grow a conscious and some balls and stop being such a twat... I am so fucking glad I don't live in America, By the way most homophobes are actually homosexual themselves - something to think about. Cham1589 2 years ago

bud dont even bother with this ignorant fuck, its not worth your time, if someone is going to be a biggot, they will be til they die RIp Lawrence KingBrodeyBitch 2 years ago

I dont agree with u billybassman21 I think every1 should be able 2 be comfortable in what they wear even if ur a guy wearing a dress,if it makes straight people uncomfortable then thats their problem & they should come 2 terms with that theirselfs we dont ask them 2 dress like that so there should be no problem & we dont care what they wear rather if it makes us comfortable or not.Life is 2 short 2 make others happy & u'll never make every1 happy anyways live 4 urself. FatelessForever1 2 years ago

4

## lawrence king i will remember

*"lol i agree. i feel bad for brandon, it's almost like hes being punished for doing somerhing good. 1 less fag in the world, the better."* iRiShplayaa13 2 years ago

**Cartermayes Inbox**

**T.miller**

**Brandon**

You're only thirteen so young! I'll pray for you and hope that you don't think you're doing a great job and end up in jail.

IRiShplayaa13

### Re: Brandon

my name isn't Brandon, its Jared and if this is about that video of the straight kid who killed his gay student, maybe the gay student shouldn't have been sexually harassing the other kid. it was bad enough the straight kid had a deep hatred for gay people to begin with, but since the faggot was hitting on him he deserved it.

**T.miller**

**Re: Re: Brandon**

I know your name isn't Brandon and you're so young that I am not going to go back and forth with you. If no one ever expresses this to you I will: Brandon had a lot to llve for and a long way to go in his life but he ended it at a young age because of homophobia. If a girl was sexually harassing him he probably wouldn't have killed her. I don't want you to (and i don't even know you) grow up and go to jail because of hatred. If you don't like any kind of people thats fine, u don't have to but you shouldn't spread hate. I feel sorry for Brandon and wish he would have told his parents and the school what was happening instead of taking matters into his own hands. As for yourself, you still have a lot to learn and a long way to go. You are one of this generations future leaders of your generation so make wise choices Grow up, get famous, be successful and remember you will meet a lot of homosexual people in this world and you might not like that but this is no one persons earth to determine who can and can not live on it.

5

YOU                                                                                            02/28/08

I LOVE THAT YOU TALKED ABOUT BEING GAY BECAUSE I LIVE IN
SPARTANBURG SOUTH CAROLINA AND THEY THINK IF YOUR
GAY U GOIN STRAIGHT TO HELL BUT I KNW GOD LOVES ME FOR
ME AND HOW I PRAISE HIM HAS NOTHIN TO DO WIT WHICH SEX
IM WIT.. YOU TOUCHED ME AND ONE MORE THING YOU ARE A
VERY BEAUTIFUL PERSON KEEP DOIN WAT U DOIN

LaShondia

Reply  Delete                                        block user    mark as spam

facebook

Email
tmiller@tmillerpoetry.com
Password
••••••••
Login
☑ Keep me logged in    Forgot your password?

## Heading out? Stay connected
Visit facebook.com on your mobile phone.

Get Facebook Mobile

## Sign Up
It's free and always will be.

| | |
|---|---|
| First Name: | |
| Last Name: | |
| Your Email: | |
| Re-enter Email: | |
| New Password: | |
| I am: | Select Sex: ↕ |
| Birthday: | Month: ↕  Day: ↕  Year: ↕ |

Why do I need to provide this?

Sign Up

Create a Page for a celebrity, band or business.

English (US)  Español  Português (Brasil)  Français (France)  Deutsch  Italiano  العربية  हिन्दी  中文(简体)  日本語  »

7

**ShowSum Courtesy'Curtis**
DOG THESE NIGGA IN THE BARBERSHOP IS SO FUCKIN FLAMBOYANT, THIS
NIGGA GON SAY "OMG TRAV YOU GOT MY THROAT SORE WIT YO PUNK
BUTT" #madhomo

October 30, 2010 at 3:16pm via Android · Like · Comment

stop going to the salon to get ur cutt FUCKBOY!
October 30, 2010 at 3:26pm · Like

**ShowSum Courtesy'Curtis** Lmao... Fuck you! They should make
all sissies be forced to get cut at the salon
October 30, 2010 at 3:28pm · Like

! LMAO NIGGA U TOO STUPID. THAT IS A GOOD
POINT THOUGH!
October 30, 2010 at 3:29pm · Like

**ShowSum Courtesy'Curtis** 4real, im buying a barber shop jus
so I can have a NO SISSIES ALLOWED sigm outside
October 30, 2010 at 3:31pm · Like

U GONE GET ASSASINATED BY ONE COMING UP
OUT UR SHOP U DO THAT LOL
October 30, 2010 at 3:41pm · Like

Write a comment...

**Natasha T. Miller**
Who did you "come out the closet" to first and what was their reaction?
January 19 at 12:44am · Like ·comment
Sarah, Leon and 2 others like this.

**Casey Johnson** I told my cousin and she thought I was playing
January 19 at 12:47am via Facebook Mobile · Like

**Keri Helper** My dad and it wasnt that bad lol
January 19 at 12:47am via Facebook Mobile · Like · 1 person

**Poetic-Bruise** My grandmother & it was really really bad
January 19 at 12:49am via Facebook Mobile · Like

**PoeticTruth Mahbehlala** My sisterhood of friends, I didn't see it as coming out tho, I was just telling them I'd fallen inlove. They were suprised to learn it was a woman but pleased to see my glow so it didn't matter much really.
January 19 at 12:50am · Like · 1 person

**Ryana Berry** To my mom lol she asked was waz I kissin boys I said no she asked was I kissin girls I said no, but the girls kissin me! Lol she almost had a car accident!
January 19 at 12:50am via Facebook Mobile · Like · 1 person

9

**L Burt** My pops, t! He said shit I love pussy too
January 19 at 12:50am · Like · 8 people

**Lynda Kd** my bother and he said he kinda knew
January 19 at 12:51am via Facebook Mobile · Like · 1 person

**Carrie Wilde** my cousin, then my homegirl... both said the same thing, "what took you so long?" lol
January 19 at 1:01am · Like · 1 person

**Antistress Jaron** My sister and she said finally and asked when did i decide to stop denying it
January 19 at 1:11am via Facebook Mobile · Like · 2 people

**Natasha T. Miller** were you denying it and if so, why? @carrie, what took you so long? @Ryana, how long did it take her to accept it? @Poeticb, how bad was it? did it forever change the relationship
January 19 at 1:16am · Like

**Poetic-Bruise** It didn't change it forever, but we didn't talk for a little over a year after she kicked me out. I was really upset so it took me a while to forgive her & it also took her a while to accept everything. she is really understanding & supportive now tho  :)
January 19 at 1:30am via Facebook Mobile · Like · 2 people

**Antistress Jaron** Yes I was denying it. I was young when i first started to accept the fact that I like girls more so than what was considered normal. And once i realized that I had feelings for females stronger than I did for males i was

10

confused. I was really into church and i was afraid of what my family would say. But after a while i decided that as long as I accept me for who I am and I love me then it doesnt matter what everyone else thinks.

January 19 at 1:34am via Facebook Mobile · Like · 1 person

**Perry Millieon** My mother, she said "I know." Lol smh

January 19 at 1:49am · Like · 1 person

**Fetima brighton** My fav kuzzin and she said me too! "Damn" let's go to the club this weekend!~We were home for springbreak/ we went to different colleges~ ♥ ink

January 19 at 1:56am via Facebook Mobile · Like · 1 person

**Ryana Berry** It didn't take long she kinda just got really possessive over me and didn't really want me to be into a woman feeling like I would forget about my #1.

January 19 at 1:59am via Facebook Mobile · Like

**Theresa Bran** My mom. She asked me "ok... did you finish your homework?"

January 19 at 3:29am · Like · 1 person

**Quinta Willis** I told my mom and she kind of didnt want to believe it. She still dont like understand it but shes coming around little by little.

January 19 at 3:31am · Like

**Temia Guignon** My best friend– but it was more that she looked at me one night and said – "Holy shit, you're in love with her aren't you?" and that was that.

When I told my mom she was completely reactionless,
when i told my dad he said he had known since I was eleven – but said he wasn't sure that i knew it yet in my teen years, and that he wanted me to tell him when

11

i was ready.
January 19 at 3:37am · Like · 1 person

**Natasha T. Miller** Did being really into church create a fear of coming out?
January 19 at 3:43am · Like

**Meka Marvins**  my sister and her grlfriend then when they got caught they told on me!!!
January 19 at 5:05am · Like

**Mindi Herine** Well, I'm not gay but bi. I told my guy first and he was a bit freaked but only because he is always afraid I'm going to leave him and he felt like now he had two sexes to worry about it. Then I told my mom and as a crazy Christian she didn't like it at all. Told me I was going to Hell and all I need is Christian counseling. It took me till I was 21 to say that I was bi and even admit it to myself because I grew up in a strict Christian family and didn't want to go to Hell.
January 19 at 5:29am · Like

**Percy Danise** I never had to say anything. My mom had read a journal entry I wrote about the person I was with at the time, and it was a female. I went to grab my journal a couple days later and I seen my mom had written me in there about the situation. She was upset but understanding. I didn't really know what to say. I went to her and we talked. Sometimes she says smart comments but I ignore them.
January 19 at 7:52am via Facebook Mobile · Like · 1 person

**Ellie** My older sister Lorren. She was going to the Marine's and she was pissed/shocked! Mind you, her ass was already gay as well! lol
January 19 at 8:08am · Like · 1 person

12

**Maine Satin** my older cuz who is like a brother. he told his mom(my aunt) whom hates the gays, she told my step mom.... who told my dad. then dad tells me " so i here u like girls" ... shcoked kid... "yeah" ... my dad in fatherly tone " make sure u graduate high school"... shoked kid"ok"
January 19 at 11:58am · Like

**Karen B** ......well,the person I had to come out to directly was my mother-she knows the type of friends I surround myself around and my ex was different from me personality wise,I took my girl to a game-my mother noticed my girl didnt pay the guys no attention and is a very attractive woman and joked and said is the girl gay-then i said yes-and we've been dating:)-she went through different emotions but now she understands its not always about the sex of the person its who makes you happy-of course i had to sum it up but I thought your topic was something i should comment on-
January 19 at 12:09pm · Like · 1 person

**Tanya Tay'a** my sister asked me after a week of shackn up wit a woman my fam was spectulating and she asked i said yes she cried and then came ova and that was that an my mom gave me the hardest time..
January 19 at 1:16pm · Like

**Antistress Jaron** Yes church instilled a fear, and for me it was because I've always been taught that being gay is a sin, that i would go to hell, that I would be looked down upon and basically cast aside. I was taught that since I was old enough to sit still in church so naturally i believed it. I was taught that men that like men and women that like women are sick, that they posess a demonic spirit that makes them that way so when i realized how i felt i was pretty scared to tell anyone else
January 19 at 1:37pm via Facebook Mobile · Like · 1 person

**Vie Of Payne Jams** I came out to my mom first when I was 12 and she didn't believe me.. She told me that I was going through a phase and I would grow out of it.. She didn't believe me until I was 20..
January 19 at 1:47pm · Like

13

**Naomi Jizz Bruner** myself....i finally stopped feeding myself bullshit looked in the mirror and said bitch your gay deal with it
January 19 at 3:02pm · Like · 3 people

**Ghana Honey Martin** I was in denail...Until I went to the club with my cousin and couldnt front anymore..lol! My mom found out on some "Hey mom this is" type stuff..She was cool until my girl left and Yep moms been tripping ever since. You would think that after 4years she would be over it but she's not... Its kinda disappointing but I have come t realize that I have to live my life for me. Every day I wake up and smile so Im Happy!
January 19 at 3:46pm · Like · 2 people

**Natasha T. Miller** My best friend and I had both developed secret girl crushes on two other "best friends" that were really girlfriends. we both knew that we both liked the both of them but it took us a while to admit that it was more than admiration that we were feeling. After a long day of conversation about how awesome we thought the two girls were i finally said to my best friend "I like such and such" and my best friend said "I like the other one" lol and from that moment forward we were openly gay to each other. No we didn't get the girls, they were already together lol.

As far as my mom I didn't have to say a word. She found an open letter that I was writing to my first love at the time and called and told my aunt that I was dating women. Word got back to me, she never asked me about it and to this day I've never had to announce my "gayness" to my family. No one questions it, my family is so accepting of my choice to date women, they treat every person that I bring home the same and its really just that simple.

I have a family full of christians but they never try to make me feel like what I'm doing is a sin: They only encourage me to keep GOD in everything that i do, be honest with others and be happy.

Thank you all for your comments. Hopefully your stories will touch the lives of other and impact a positive "coming out" movement.
February 2 at 11:23pm · Like

Write a comment...

14

**ShowSum Courtesy'Curtis**
IF YOU ASK ME FAGGOTS SHOULD NOT BE ALLOWED TO WORK IN PUBLIC!
October 15, 2010 at 8:37pm via Android · Like · Comment

Lol.. where should they work then?..
October 15, 2010 at 8:43pm · Like

and i think all trannys should be shipped to homo island but what are u gonna do
October 15, 2010 at 8:46pm · Like

DONT ASK DONT TELL!!!!,,,LOL
October 15, 2010 at 8:47pm · Like

U don't have to ask, u can already tell nowadays...
October 15, 2010 at 8:49pm · Like · 👍 1 person

**ShowSum Courtesy'Curtis** Under ground, caves, forests,deserts, and islands with little to no population
October 15, 2010 at 8:50pm · Like

lol
October 15, 2010 at 8:50pm · Like

**ShowSum Courtesy'Curtis** Trannies should be crucified!
October 15, 2010 at 8:50pm · Like · 👍 2 people

ye they r the worst! uggh especially the ones that look believable u cant even enjoy a fat ass from a distance no more u gotta do a thourough walk by before I can be excited now :(
October 15, 2010 at 8:52pm · Like · 👍 1 person

LOL @ under ground...
October 15, 2010 at 8:53pm · Like

15

**Natasha T. Miller**

Question: Heterosexual men and Heterosexual women, how would you feel and or what would you do if a homosexual man or woman made a sexual advance or became openly flirtatious with you?

February 3 at 5:00pm · Like ·
Adrianne likes this.

**Shearton vall** I have had this happen, and I just tell them that I'm not homosexual
February 3 at 5:01pm · Like

**Jamer Hars** Give em the "time out" and "hold fast" look... and explain....i'm good... , but years ago... probably a different story.... but growth is a wonderful thing...
February 3 at 5:02pm · Like · 1 person

**Vigel kson** As long as i know who i an... I'm cool with it.. It's all about being comfortable with your self.
Greatest Love ever.
February 3 at 5:03pm · Like

**Mindi Herine** The same way you would turn down a straight person...
February 3 at 5:04pm · Like · 2 people

**Niema Jackson** Tell them im not n2 women. I have gay female friends and theyre just as cooj as my strait friends. As long as ur secure wit ur sexuality then there should b no problems.
February 3 at 5:04pm · Like

16

**Lah Ex** ...I wouldn't take offense to it until the advancements or passes became disrespectful AFTER I've directly informed them I am not homosexual and have no interest in them in that way
February 3 at 5:21pm · Like · 2 people

**Brandi Johns** Take it as a compliment... they think im hot! lol I would do like the other young lady said, turn them down as i do ppl of the opposite sex
February 3 at 5:32pm · Like · 2 people

**Drianne Lee** In a nice way, say thanks but no thanks! :)
February 3 at 5:36pm · Like

**Amirea Ram** flattered. I've never been hit on by a woman, I'm feeling real inadequate over here.
February 3 at 5:39pm · Like · 1 person

**Drianne Lee** I agree w/ Amirea...flattered. Feels validating 2 b hit on by both genders! Though uncomfortable @ the moment, when I walk away, I'm like fuck yeah! Even the bitches want me!...then the more times I get hit on, I feel insecure wondering if I give off the wrong vibe
February 3 at 6:01pm · Like · 2 people

**LaToria's Cookies** i wud tell them thanks for being interested but im not on that level and wud b impressed that a woman wud look @ me like that.. Its happened 2 me plenty of times i just smile an keep it movin as if they were a man:)
February 3 at 6:13pm · Like

17

**Amirea Ram** LOL...Drianne, you hit it on the head, lady! I think my hetero vibe is overpowering.
February 3 at 6:19pm · Like

**Sheka Rhodes** i do believe the kick is called a roundhouse.
February 3 at 6:31pm · Like

**Niema Jackson** I agree with the ladies. Because i have both gay friends and family members i am often n the company of gay women who hit on me. It just doesn't bother me. Like i said b4 im secure enough n my sexuality 2 b flattered by their advances. It means nothing more 2 me than a compliment
February 3 at 6:34pm · Like

**Asul Rebel** 2 be honest I would feel like I don't want anotha male attracted 2 me. I would politely tell them "This ain't that kind of party". . . Now if they make sexual advances 2 the point pass flirtin when there touchin or grabbin shit they ain't got no business touchin? . . . Then ima have ta commense 2 whoopin their assssss!
February 3 at 7:33pm · Like

**Niema Jackson** Well of corse. Flirting and violating are 2 dffrnt things. Touchn and grabbing is out of line be it man or woman. As long as im not being physically violated im ok. The flirting doesnt bother me
February 3 at 7:42pm · Like · 1 person

**Mila Willfords** i wanna comment on this so bad,T. but........... im not heterosexual... LOLOL!!♥
February 3 at 8:07pm · Like · 1 person

**Dexter Bleu** ive had some interesting encounters with this and i

18

simply laughed and said "nah i'm straight" with the guys anyway but i am a lesbian by trade sometimes lol...some gay men ive come across were so feminine energy wise i almost forgot they were males

February 3 at 8:10pm · Like

**Kyla Bron** I feel the same way I would if a hetero-man made an advance towards me. its all attraction!

February 3 at 8:12pm · Like

**Niema Jackson** Whats stoppn u mila. Make ur comment! Tel us what u got 2 say. We're all adults. Any1 who gets offended shouldnt b n this discussion n the 1st place

February 3 at 8:22pm · Like

**Omar Dale** Wouldn't bother me people have the right to admire. I would only be bothered if they continued after I tell them I'm not interested. That bothers me with a woman.

February 3 at 9:06pm · Like · 2 people

**Mindi Herine** @Mila– Well technically I'm not either... well not completely but I think the answer is easy. Only a homophobe would feel anything but flattered really I think. I'm bi and love that not only do both sexes appeal to me but I can appeal to both sexes as well. My problem comes from the fact that I've only been with men so I get flustered when it happens with a woman especially since I;m in a committed relationship with a man.

February 3 at 10:04pm · Like

**Niema Jackson** @mindi i agree with u about homophobes. Now u said ur bi. Im curious u said u've only been with men. Now how does that wrk? Strait women like myself have only been with men how r u diffrent frm us. R u really bisexual or just a freak. Im comfused

February 3 at 10:15pm · Like

19

**Darren Brax** Truthfully...I would definitely feel uncomfortable,I would definitely let them know what was up,but as long as the line isn't crossed we're good

February 3 at 10:15pm · Like

**Mindi Herine** @Niema– Well put it this way before you had been with a man did you know you were straight. I'm willing to bet that you did. I personally find women much more appealing and fantasize about being with one. At the same time though I love my guy and enjoy having sex with him, I also find other men attractive. If I had a chance with a woman and the permission from my guy I would in a heartbeat so yes I'm bisexual and excuse me but I'm not a "freak". lol! You and others may not like to hear this, I don't know but I do watch porn and when I do i watch lesbian porn as far as I'm concerned I've already got a man so I watch the other.

February 3 at 10:30pm · Like · 1 person

**Niema Jackson** Oh ok. I just didnt undrstnd hw that works. As a matter of fact ur bet is dead on the money as a lil girl ive loved men. Growing up i loved everything about them. I couldnt personally imagine myself wit a chick nor do i desire 1 but i have a friend i grew up wit who loves women and i respect her choice. I also have a cuzn who use 2 love men but had her heart broken by a few loosers now she wit a chick. Im ok wit that but part of me feels like its 4 attn. How do u go back and 4th btwn men and women r u confused. And hw do u knw u want 2b wit a chick 4real if u only been wit men. I mean i look @ chicks all the time i think r beautiful but im nt attracted 2 them. I

February 3 at 10:47pm · Like · 1 person

**Niema Jackson** And how do u know ur actually bi verses curious? My cousin said she's gay but she still sleeps wit men. She been wit both genders so now which 1 of yall is bi and which is confused

February 3 at 10:50pm · Like

**Mindi Herine** Honestly, it is hard to explain. My mom is a lesbian and obviously she slept with at least a man. In case she was burned by several men

20

and fell for a woman. I don't know if it is because she is honestly gay or because she fell in love with a woman or if it was because she swore off men. Like i said I dream about sleeping with a woman and doing everything you would do with a man with a woman. I also have gay friends who can see it, like they're gaydar goes off kind of thing. Most people swing more one way than the other. On a scale of 1–10 of how gay I am I'd say I'm around an 8 (so more gay than not). I hope that helps.

I would say you're friend is confused/curious or bi. If she were purely gay then she would only sleep with women. For some people it is extremely confusing, nevewracking, scary, etc...
February 3 at 10:54pm · Like

**Niema Jackson** Oh ok. I guess i may never understand no matter how much u school me. Ill never knw y a woman would want 2b with anything but a man but hey its ur life not meant 4 me 2 judge. If u gne live it: live it 2 the fullest. U do u ima do men lol. Alrite hun nice chattn wit u. Hope i didnt say anythng 2 offend u or any1 else i was taught: if u wanna knw ask. Goodnite
February 3 at 11:02pm · Like · 2 people

**Mindi Herine** Good night and thank you for being very polite, sweet and nice about it all, I understand the need to ask and try to understand things. We may never understand some things but as long as it doesn't create a barrier or bigotry things are good!
February 3 at 11:08pm · Like

**James Neilson** I would be flattered...
February 4 at 12:26am · Like

**Omar Dale** I would say though, that although i would not be bothered by it, I wouldn't be too critical of someone that was uneasy about it. some folks don't like the idea of anyone they are not attracted to being attracted to them, it goes beyond any various ways of being sometimes
February 4 at 1:45am · Like · 2 people

**Levia Tru** Sexuality is not a gay or straight attribute. . Its both. My opinion is everyone can be either or. Some are just more honest an intuned with what they like rather than allow society to dictate an suppress their natural attraction towardz another. Scientifically we were all female at da 1st stages of life cycle LOL Rt

February 4 at 9:30am · Like · 1 person

**Mindi Herine** @Levia– That is like the Kinsey scale. Kinsey said that there are very few people who are strictly straight or strictly gay or right down the middle. He said if there were a line starting at straight and ending in gay most people would fall somewhere in between the two ends but not directly in the middle either. And the last thing you said is absolutely true. :)

February 4 at 10:48am · Like · 1 person

**Vigel Kson** I couldn't be made because someone spoke there mind... Sexuality dose not have a look... it's just an attraction to that the person!!!

February 4 at 12:10pm · Like · 1 person

**Levia Tru** Word @mindi

February 4 at 6:47pm · Like · 1 person

Write a comment...

THIS HOE ASS NIGGA WALKIN AROUND IN WRANGLERS WIT THE ENTIRE KNEES CUT OUT AND OPEN TOE SANDALS.... SMH THE LIBRARY IS A PLACE YOU COME TO LEARN, RELAXAN WORK, NOT WORSHIP RAINBOWS AND OTHER FAGGOTY HOMO TRADEMARKS. IT SEEM LIKE NOWADAYS NO MATTER WHERE U GO, U CANT ESCAPE THESE BASTARDS!

July 19, 2010 at 12:22pm via Mobile Web · Like · Comment

🖒 3 people like this.

 Me & him are matching I have that same shit on (Not wranglers tho lol)
July 19, 2010 at 12:33pm · Like

 why u aint come thru so we can work!!!
July 19, 2010 at 12:34pm · Like

 lmao I looked and I couldnt find the word Faggoty in the dictionary
July 19, 2010 at 12:52pm · Like

 ShowSum Courtesy°Curtis Lol, its cool for u but that shit aint right for dude...
July 19, 2010 at 12:53pm · Like

 lmao @ David....N I think you need counseling Curt you may be suffering from Homophobia
July 19, 2010 at 12:54pm · Like

23

## New message

**To**  Enter a friend's name or email address

**Message**  CHAPTER2
We all want approval and we all first want approval from the
ones we love. When your family knows and accepts, you feel
so much better about being, anything. I believe that even the
ones who pretend not to care about family acceptance still
spend their lives, to a degree, trying to get a level of
acceptance from their family consciously or sub-consciously.
When your family has said yes or you can, the no or the no
you cants of the world seem less important. There is almost
no greater pain than the pain you feel when your blood, your
flesh, your providers, your all you've ever known and want to
make proud in this world tells you that your life choices or
love choices are wrong and that the doors of their hearts are
closed to you.

**Send**  Cancel

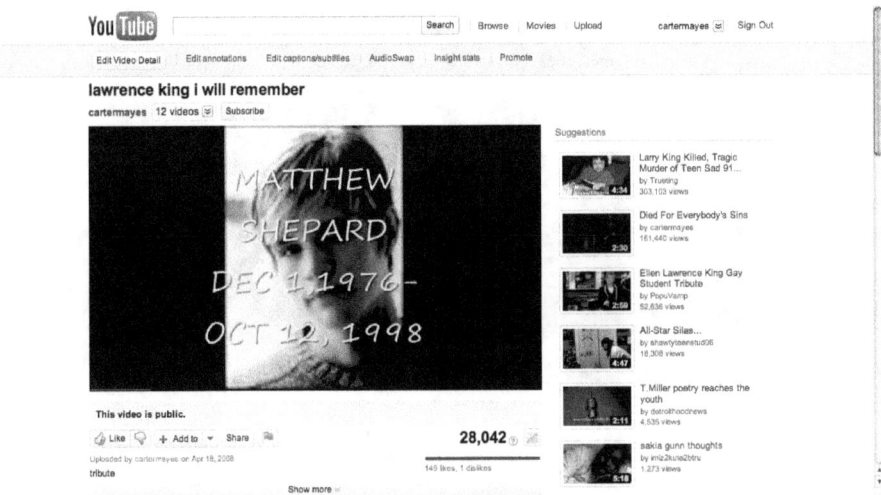

My daughter is professing homosexuality. It is so hard for me to watch this "tribute". I hate what happened to Matthew, Scott, Larry and many others I can not name. I hate pain experienced by any human being perpetrated on them from the void place of evil others. I do not accept the homosexual lifestyle. It would break my heart for my own child to suffer due to someone elses hate of someone I love some very dearly. God help us all. earthlycolorbrown 1 year ago

You should accept your daughter's life choices. She will look to you for support and you should be there for her whenever she needs it. Read the book "Prayers for Bobby" and/or watch the movie that was played on A&E. That might help you understand where another mother didn't accept it and lost her son. At some point she will need you, and I hope you will be there for her, and any other person who needs someone to talk to, about anything. tazdog8585 1 year ago

tears down my face... for sakia gunn, it's a shame what happened 2 that yung girl.. all because of HOMOSEXUALITY. it sickens me to see the VIOLENCE that happens to the gay community/LGBTQ, all because they like the same fckn gender! like wtf yo! like why can't we live in PEACE, why can't we live our lives without bein JUDGED bcuz of our preference? the gay community DESERVES just as much RESPECT as the str8 community. Xpeechez 1 year ago 4

faggots are gay iMxth3xbossx3000 1 year ago

@iMxth3xbossx3000 straight people are murderers! philby74 1 year ago

27

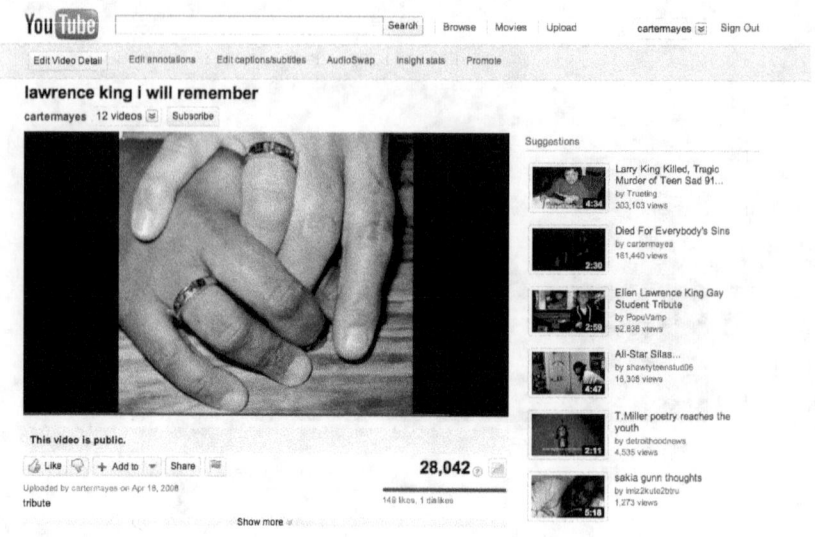

I dont understand y ppl have to take out on gay ppl..so at they like their own gender wat makes them soo much more different than straight..i myself am 12 and straight but becuz i have heard bout this kid dying it changes my whole veiw of saying the word gay and how much it effects ppl.i never realized how harsh ppl can be just becuz of one little simple thing. we are all united in a way wether were black, white straight gay it doesn't matter, we're all untied in a way
sp0rt5gir1 2 years ago

is this the world that we want?because i don't want this world.we have to learn to accept people.who cares if he is gay or black the only thing that we should care if he or she is a good person. eleni25lostfan 2 years ago

I am a straight female who happened to see you video somehow by being linked while looking for coverage of the McCain RNC speech! I had no idea Larry King was killed in a town I live less than one hour from, 7 months ago. Your video solidifed for me the reasons in which we must VOTE Obama-Biden in 08, we need change. We as a country must learn to accept everyone as humans, as Americans not based on race, or sexual orientation. I'm just sorry it was to late for Lawrence King. Thank you katee708 2 years ago 4

RIP Lawrence King... we're sad for what happened... I am also gay and things have to change... ppl have to stop being jerks... we're not diff. than anyone else, we juss like a person of the same gender..but we feel pain, cry, laugh, like anyother...think about it before judging a gay muriloluvusa 2 years ago

28

**See who's here**

Friends and industry peers you know. Celebrities you watch. Businesses you frequent. Find them all on Twitter.

**Top Tweets** View all ›

Mike_FTW Text QUAKE to 98734 to help the poor souls who spilled their Blue Bottle coffee on their G-Star Jeans in the SF quake of 2011.
2 hours ago · · retweet · favorite

GeorgeTakei An fascinating step toward Scotty really being able to beam me up! http://ow.ly/4CKbq As my fans say on Twitter: #Nerdgasm
2 hours ago · · retweet · favorite

johnwbradley CEO of company that makes Nutella dies in cycling accident. Twice the sad. http://wrd.tw/gq1KkC
2 hours ago · · retweet · favorite

Find out how some of your favorite people use Twitter.

**invincibleDET** Invincible
homophobe unfollow day...once again...especially sucks to unfollow people who you stand in solidarity with but they hate on who you are smh.
1 hour ago

**facebook**

Email
tmiller@tmillerpoetry.com
Password
••••••••
Login
☑ Keep me logged in     Forgot your password?

## Heading out? Stay connected
Visit facebook.com on your mobile phone.

Get Facebook Mobile

## Sign Up
It's free and always will be.

First Name:
Last Name:
Your Email:
Re-enter Email:
New Password:

I am:  Select Sex: ♦

Birthday:  Month: ♦  Day: ♦  Year: ♦
Why do I need to provide this?

Sign Up

Create a Page for a celebrity, band or business.

English (US)  Español  Português (Brasil)  Français (France)  Deutsch  Italiano  العربية  हिन्दी  中文(简体)  日本語  »

31

**Natasha T. Miller**
Have you ever or do you ever pray for a "straight" kid? If yes, y?

September 21, 2010 at 12:04pm · Like ·comment
Jazzer likes this.

**Terry Wilkinson** I plan to love my kids no matter who or what they become. If people pray for a straight kid, its because [A] they're homophobic or [B] they feel being anything other than straight is "easier"...which is weird, because life isn't meant to be that way.
September 21, 2010 at 12:10pm · Like

**Mia Fall God Hill** A striaght boy yes definitly I have no problem with gay men but me personally I wouldn't want my son to be gay I want him to get girls and have kids and a wife its just the masculine thing I love in men...female idk it don't bother me as much...
September 21, 2010 at 12:11pm · Like

**Mia Fall God Hill** But I will love them reguarless...
September 21, 2010 at 12:11pm · Like

**Darren Brax** Wow,I never prayed on my child's sexual preference...to tell the truth I would want my children to have children of their own and be in a heterosexual relationship,but if they end up being homosexual I have no control over that,they're still our children and we should accept what they have chosen for their lives,when I was in the streets my mother never turned her back on me no matter what I did and as parents we need to be there for our children no matter what
September 21, 2010 at 12:11pm · Like · 1 person

32

**Mia Fall God Hill** Oh and I didn't actually pray but thought about it a couple times
September 21, 2010 at 12:13pm · Like

**Tammy Holy Tutter** I have a 6yr old son and I have never prayed for him to be straight. As a parent of course it is a concern but instead of praying that he does not end up that way I pray for him daily that the Lord will continue to keep him, love him, cover him, release His favor, mercy and grace over his life, that He continues to order his steps and allow him to have a sound heart and a sound mind, rebuking the enemy and any negative thing that tries to attach itself to him because at the end of the day...its not my will or my sons will but its about Gods will for his life. So I trust in Him no matter what He may allow to take place in His life that the end results will line up according to His word.
September 21, 2010 at 12:47pm · Like · 6 people

**Darren Brax** @Tammy...love it,because that's what it's really about,out of all the responses yours is the realest and most down to earth,keep God first and put all your worries on His shoulders and he'll take care of the rest
September 21, 2010 at 12:51pm · Like

**Stephen Suten** "i'll tell her to be tri-sexual, to try anything, to sleep with, fight with, pray with anyone..." from Nichole Blackmen "Daughter"

Does it really matter?
September 21, 2010 at 1:25pm · Like

**Tammy Holy Tutter** Its nothing wrong with being "tri-sexual" if thats what you prefer; just be ready to face the risks/consequences of your explorations or choices. In life its said we will lose some and win some which is a true statement but if I can keep from letting the opportunity of a lost arise I would rather do that. Its somethings we just dont have to do or go through but being "tri-sexual" will open up a level of exposure that a person should be open in every aspect to endure.
September 21, 2010 at 1:37pm · Like · 1 person

33

**Stephen Suten** Oops left off this part:

"just as long as she feels something."
September 21, 2010 at 1:59pm · Like

**Naomi Jizz Bruner** Ive often thought about this at the risk of sounding like a hypocrite ive prayed for my son to be heterosexual many times as a lesbian and an activist Im extremely aware of heterosexual privilege , the dangers ,hatred, etc. that gay men face....I want my son to have the best life possible and in my opinion life straight men have it easier
September 21, 2010 at 2:06pm · Like

**Lory Height**  i pray for people. and that kids everywhere grow up to know love in some way shape or form. from a boy. from a girl. from friends. from family. or from complete strangers. as long as they find that love that's all i think really matters.
September 21, 2010 at 3:00pm · Like

**Darla Miller** I don't think it's about straight/gay or any of that when your praying I think/know not for me anyway it's about me having love for that person and that goes for drinking, smoking, druging, robbing, jailed, mentally impaired, sick in the body ect..... any and all other things you can come up with or think up!!!!! why on GODS green earth would that even matter? to each his own we all have grown up with some sort of gay/lesbian/hetero people around us but when you get a certain age nobody can make choices for you and no one can be judged for you either, all I can say is what ever you choose I guess I/we have to be happy with that!!!!! and love you for WHO you are even though sometimes we may not be in agreement with YOUR choice!!
September 21, 2010 at 6:36pm · Like

**Natasha T. Miller** I see the beauty in every response here. I use to think about all of the things I didn't want my kids to be, based on all of the things other people are; hateful above all, then I was blessed with a nephew. I watch him smile, I watch him be happy and I think about all of the happiness that my fear once, almost stripped him of and I feel awful. Being gay is hard but so is being black and so is being woman, being Jewish, being famous, being Caucasian, being loved, being God and being human. To feel love is to be loved for who and what you truly are. Controlling our kids seem so much easier than controlling ourselves but really what we are doing is assisting with the loss of control of themselves. God is love and when it comes to our children, that's' all we should pray for.

September 21, 2010 at 11:54pm · Like · 1 person

Write a comment....

**Thank you! You saved my life!**

Dear T.Miller.

Today, I was in the library at school,I logged on to FB and saw your stat. You had posted a link to your youtube video (which was too funny).I went through your videos and I was in awe!! I cried like a baby! T. Miller,everything in your poem was like my past and present. All my life,I've dated men,who have beat me, lowered my self worth and made me feel like scum! I dealt with it because, in my heart, I knew I was a lesbian but my family would never accept me for the real me. I've been touched by men in my family, never had my "father" around. When I was in 10th grade, I wanted to die, because I knew that when I saw a "stud" how it made me feel inside. My mom was not having it! I wanted to end my life!! I let a man use my body,because it was the "normal" thing to do! I've hurt for so many years!! Because of your words I feel free! I can't live for my family, I have to live for Keila. I'm not out here looking for flings, I just want to give my all to another beautiful woman.I see "studs" all up and threw EMU,but I never approach them, If you could only feel what I feel when I'm around one! Lol oh boy!

You have no idea the impact that you have had on my life. Your truly amazing! I respect and adore you! You've saved my life, I can live now! I'm ok with being gay, I'm not hurting! GOD loves me too! You helped me to see this! I'm good! You die for my sins,I die for yours! Thank you! (Tear) xo

**Natasha T. Miller**

**Why are people more bothered by a man with a man than a woman with a woman?**

September 10, 2010 at 12:47pm · Like ·comment

   2 others like this.

**Nika IdoMe Clay** its just plain ol nasty

September 10, 2010 at 12:51pm · Like

**Natasha T. Miller** what do you think is nasty about it @Idome?

September 10, 2010 at 12:52pm · Like

**Osteria Mae** We live in a patriarchal society that prides itself on maintaining masculinity, male/male intimacy debunks this and female/female intimacy further perpetuates their suppression of us... This is my Marxist review of the matter :)

September 10, 2010 at 12:53pm · Like · 4 people

**Nika IdoMe Clay** idk maybe the thought of 2 men bumping bootys just don't sit well wit me...when you think of a "MAN" you think masculine and for them to be doing each other is just nasty

September 10, 2010 at 12:54pm · Like

**Bastia onlyboneme** Because of the pentration, for me. That is a life changing experience, just ask any down low brother who got his cherry popped doing a five yr bid in Jackson and came home 'different'....

September 10, 2010 at 12:54pm · Like

**Eli Gray** society has made lesbians "fashionable". Things like "girls gone wild" and playboy are geared towards straight men who may not want to see a naked man in the picture. two attractive women is more sexually appealing (even though, if both the attractive women are lesbian, neither one of them is interested in the straight man). The constant shoving down our throats of lesbians being "hot" has made it ok and more normal than two gay men who are still called "queer" and "faggot" by the ignorant
September 10, 2010 at 12:55pm · Like · 3 people

**Natasha T. Miller** If you are disgusted by tjhe sexual acts of a man with another man, do you think that its fair for a heterosexual to be disgusted by the sexual acts of women on women?
September 10, 2010 at 12:58pm · Like · 1 person

**Level Detroit** Aesthetic judement
September 10, 2010 at 12:58pm · Like

**Dana Iam** Double standards suck! I think society said ok we see lesbians are considered sexy and marketable we accept you now but we havent accepted gay men because we cant sell/make money off of that life style ...yet.
September 10, 2010 at 12:59pm · Like

**Shearton vall** I think it depends on who you talk to. Some men may not be as taken aback by two women and some women may not be as taken aback by two men
September 10, 2010 at 1:01pm · Like

**Bastia onlyboneme** Also two women are soft, whereas men are hard. Two hard things dont evoke an image of passion or sensuality. True it is a double standard but we as ppl are visual. I say to teach his own, as long as u are honest with urself and others.

38

September 10, 2010 at 1:11pm · Like · 1 person

**Delmar Quivens** Sadly there are some men who are intimidated by other mens sexual appendages and so seeing two women together is not a threat. Not to mention some men have sexual urges toward other men and are confused or upset by it. Those men will lash out at gay men as a way to justify themselves. And then of course you have the people who feel cheated because a good looking woman or man is attracted to the same sex and that means they have no chance of getting them. I was interested in a girl once who starting dating women and I didnt know what to do. The girl she was interested in was fine, funny and great to be around... I didnt know how or if I could compete with that. My first feeling was anger about her wanting a woman instead of a man and then I just realized I was jealous. I had to grow up.
September 10, 2010 at 1:12pm · Like

**Tae Que** I agree with michael, it depends on who and where they were raised whether in an accepting and open- minded family they would be very open with any lifestyle or just ignorant and biased.

We should not forget the fact that even in the LGBTQ community there are closed-minded ppl that do not accept transgendered folks and bisexual women.....
September 10, 2010 at 1:17pm · Like · 1 person

**MrsCartier** Well,,To Be Honest!!!...NO ONE SHOULD JUDGE, IT'S JUST THAT EVERYONE POINT OF VEIW IS DIFFERENT AND MOST TIMES PLP ARE JUST ALWAYS JUDGEMENTAL ABOUT EVERYTHING,, BUT I DON'T KNOW WHY PLP JUST CAN'T ACCEPT SOMEONE FOR WHO THEY ARE!!!
September 10, 2010 at 1:44pm · Like

**Michel Rags** I think because girls are all soft and sensual and dudes are all like YEAH DOG and real rough and shit so people be like i'd rather see two pretty sensual beings being sexually interactive than 2 rough hairy men lol And just because WOMEN are BEAUTIFUL to EVERYONE, like a man isnt traditionally looked at as beautiful by MEN AND women. But women are looked at as beautiful by women and men traditionally. So its just more appeasing to the eye for the MAJORITY of people I know. But either way it goes its wrong,

39

because everybody is equal and should be able to do what they choose to do with who ever they choose to do it with.
September 10, 2010 at 1:44pm · Like · 1 person

**Shearton vall** @Tae: Thanks ;)
@Michel: I was laughing at "YEAH DOG" LOL
September 10, 2010 at 1:47pm · Like

**Tae Que** "Yeah dog" anytime! Lol
September 10, 2010 at 1:48pm · Like

**Daruis Genius Waleh** Men are more accustomed to seeing women being "intimate" with each other. Whatever their orientaion is,we see women kiss,caress,hug for long periods of time,go to the bathroom together,get naked with each other,play in each other's hair,express feelings about each others specific body parts etc. So its not a huge stretch to us mentally for them taking the next step. Now,Men usually require SPACE between one another,almost all of those actions mentioned above MAY quite possibly end up a FIST Fight if expressed by 2 heterosexual guys! Also,ppl will always have a problem w/things they THINK are "different" ...
September 10, 2010 at 1:49pm · Like · 3 people

**Darren Brax** I don't want to offend anyone...I accept those who are homosexual and have friends who concider themselves homosexual,but do not agree with neither,my friends talk about me all the time because I was the only one who didn't like lesbians even if they were the two sexiest women on earth,I just don't think it's attractive,but since I am a man I really don't like the fact that two men are sexual with each other,it's just discusting concidering the way they have sex...through the rear end...the part of the body that releases feces...nasty!
September 10, 2010 at 1:59pm · Like

**Clarence J. Willamson** one word..."penetration"
September 10, 2010 at 2:25pm · Like

40

**Eria Houston** Oh lordy, lordy. Do you know how many heterosexual couples engage in anal sex? As in sex...through the booty hole...where POO comes from!? (grasps her pearls) Come one people. We've figured out why it makes people more comfy to see two lush, lovely women swappin spit. That's kind of common sense, though some might argue that there are plenty of sensual, soft, BEAUTIFUL men in this world too.

All's I know is if you're shocked by the act of penetration alone– male to male– think about some of the kooky shit hetero folks get themselves into. Step into some of the bedrooms I've been in and I'll show you an ABOMINATION. Gay sex aint got shit on half the nasty thangs hetero folks do without being chastized or judged because...well...that's the way it should be.

If it feels good, do it... Long as everyone's of age... And there are no unsuspecting animals involved...
September 10, 2010 at 2:37pm · Like

**Tae Que** Amen eria, don't hate, participate!
September 10, 2010 at 2:46pm · Like

**Darren Brax** I agree with you Eria,but all of thee above discusts me even the kiny shyt heterosexuals do,I just don't agree with any of it
September 10, 2010 at 3:05pm · Like

**Bastia onlyboneme** Its all a matter of perception, no one holds the right to judge the other and no one has it all figured out. Ppl should be free to love as they please without being frowned upon by someone with nothing better to do than speculate and comment on somebody else's kool aid
September 10, 2010 at 3:17pm · Like

**Eria Houston** Wait, who's page are we on again?...Sorry, I just had to. Love you T.
Facebook must be a terrifying place for you, Darren.
September 10, 2010 at 3:29pm · Like

**Jarred Buzilo** Eri is forbidding me from commenting. You may send your gratitude to her directly.
September 10, 2010 at 3:38pm · Like

**Michel Rags** Sex is just sex at the end of the day, its just who you choose to watch, or participate with. Althought I would say that weight is a favtor. Cause biggie smalls and big pun together would've made ANYONE's stomach crumble into a million pieces and then if Monique and Nell Carter had sex I woud've said the same shit lol so there is nothing wrong with sexual orientation but you can make an argument for just things that look kinda nasty together. Cottage cheese and blood/Whitney and Bobby/Alicia Keys and Swizz Beatz' nose. And so on and so on.
September 10, 2010 at 3:57pm · Like · 1 person

**Bastia onlyboneme** leave it to michel to bring the comic relief... lol Nell carter? you had to dig deep for that one
September 10, 2010 at 4:00pm · Like

**Michel Rags** yeah thats what she said! lol
September 10, 2010 at 4:06pm · Like

**Clarence J. Willamson** I agree completely with you, Eria...as a male hetero, growing up completely immersed in a homophobic society, I had to first recognize my homophobia, which was only directed at male-male relations, as being a problem. Once I got past that, I had to get to the core of my homophobia. It was then I realized that I was in fear of being penetrated. Now that I have addressed that fear...male-male relations seem just as normal as female-female relations. Well...as normal as they can be, given mainstream society's judgement and damnation.
September 10, 2010 at 5:11pm · Like

**Natasha T. Miller** I love you guys, I can't wait until I get some time to really join in. :)
September 10, 2010 at 5:12pm · Like

**Tae Que** Michel you crack me up and since you put it so beautifully I cannot agree more!!! And eria I'm on our side girl!
September 10, 2010 at 5:18pm · Like

**Natasha T. Miller** The most interesting part of this discussion is the overwhelming response to sex and not homosexuality. when asked why bothered by two men together and not two women together, people automatically respond to the bedroom interactions. most people can't stand the sight/thought of anal sex, but honestly, unless you purchase gay porn or peep through windows and watch gay men have sex, or engage in sexual activities with homosexual men; you never get to see that part.There is no fence to strattle here, you either accept homosexuality or you don't. you don't hate "fags" but love lesbians: you hate homosexuality but you find pleasure in watching two women interact sexually, and that is not defined as homosexuality. As a lesbian woman I find it offensive that another lesbian woman would entertain such ignorance and hate by not agreeing with the harmless sexual preference of another human being but ask for her own acceptance.

To the surprise of many, not all lesbians perform oral sex and not all gay men participate in anal sex. life and sex are all personal preference and maybe if we stopped thinking about what people do for each other sexually and start noticing what people do for each other spiritually and emotionally our stereotypes would broaden or carry less ignorance .I often hear people sum of their thought on homosexuality by saying "what they do in their bedrooms is their business." failing to realize that love is not about bedrooms and why cant what we do everywhere be our business.

I think this conversation is not about covering your eyes but adjusting your hearts. Once when we realize that we too are being accepted, we'll open our spirits more to acceptance.

Thank you all.
September 11, 2010 at 3:53pm · Like · 1 person

43

**Asta Marcy** As much as I love my homosexual friends I feel awkward & creepy when I see either man with a man or woman with a woman if it's anything more than a simple kiss or hand holding because it's so opposite what I would do. So I wonder if any of them feel the same way about us heterosexuals when they see us?

I think in general people feel like women are possibly just experimenting and may "get past it" while guys have had the reputation of being pedophiles too so maybe they think that is a truth and not a myth therby making women less threatening (not to mention guys who fantasize about having 2 women at once) since most heterosexuals don't know or understand much about homosexuality.
September 12, 2010 at 3:41pm · Like

Write a comment...

## New message

**To**  Enter a friend's name or email address

**Message**

CHAPTER3
On this earth we are distanced by continents, by countries, by states, by cities, by towns, by families, by households, by bedrooms, by dinner tables, by cars, by clothes, by aisles, by everything, or at least by everything that can be touched. You can not touch air therefore it can not separate you, I once had this exact thought about God...I thought God was in your spirit, in your healing, in your emotions, in your thoughts and in your love so therefore he or she or it could never separate you from other people. I once thought that the purpose of God was to help us feel each other without touching, bring us closer together without moving and to help us love and understand each other with or without knowing one another, but for a large majority, I think Gods true purpose has gotten lost in translation. God and Religion are now our biggest dividers. We war in the name of our God, we shut out in the name of our God, we lose touch in the name of our God, We judge in the name of our God, we divide, and do the opposite of everything that we are suppose to be doing in the name of our God...Religion can be very dangerous when you are close to it but far from the purpose of its creation.

**Send**  Cancel

**lawrence king i will remember**

cartermayes   12 videos ⌄   Subscribe

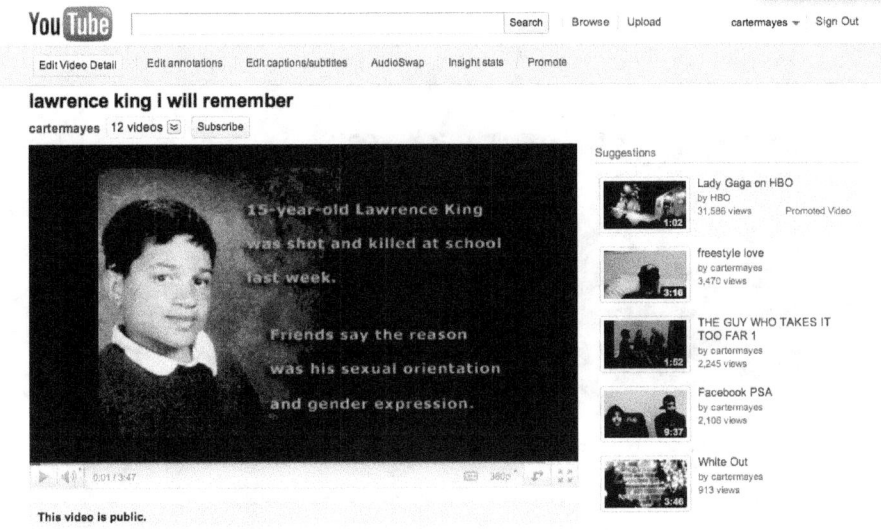

Suggestions

Lady Gaga on HBO
by HBO
31,586 views    Promoted Video

freestyle love
by cartermayes
3,470 views

THE GUY WHO TAKES IT TOO FAR 1
by cartermayes
2,245 views

Facebook PSA
by cartermayes
2,108 views

White Out
by cartermayes
913 views

This video is public.

## Top Comments

ANDYDIVA - So you'd beat up/kill a child. You're worthless, cowardly bigot boy.   cutedyke2 2 years ago 30

## All Comments (278)

Baskuk- it is not a Satan to like the same sex. The bible says god had 2 fathers. God will not have made us if he would of disapprove of our sexuality. People should be proud for who they Really are.

THATS WHAT OUR FUCKING FAGG SOCIETY ITS TEACHING KIDS THAT IS OK TO BE AN ARSE FUCKER , GO TO HELL NOW AND GIVE PLANTY OF BLOWJOBS TO THE SATAN ,YOU WILL BE SATANS VALENTINE baskuk 8 months ago

@baskuk its teaching kids that its ok to murder another human being? No, that's what you religitards are teaching kids idaman12345 7 months ago

you guys are a bunch of butt faggots. God killed the butt faggots of sodom and gamorra, and he almost killed the butt faggots of another place till jonah told them to stop being butt faggots. Pray he spares you. dukiedu 8 months ago

@dukiedu god isnt real idaman12345 7 months ago

This is amazing! I can't stop watching it. When Larry King was murdered, my heart simply broke. Nobody should have to die because of the people they love or the way they express their gender. ByteOfPi 11 months ago

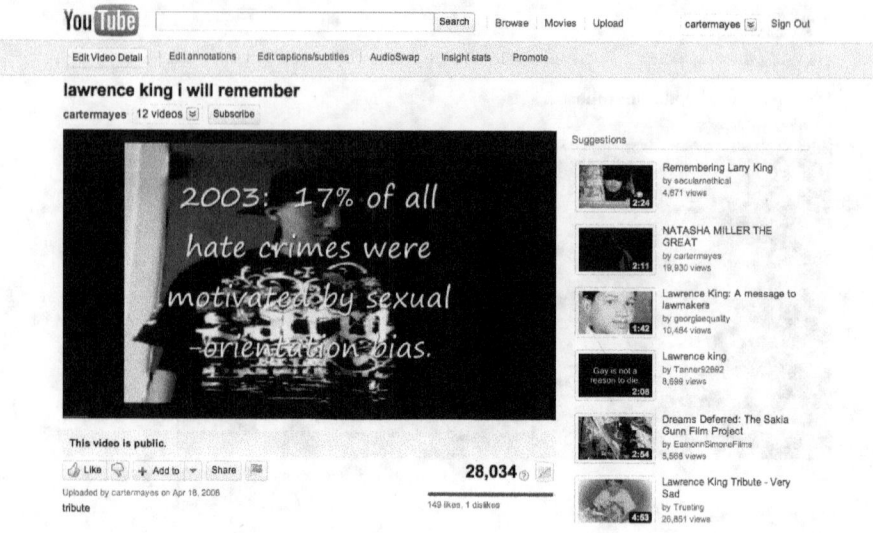

**lawrence king i will remember**

cartermayes 12 videos | Subscribe

2003: 17% of all hate crimes were motivated by sexual orientation bias.

Suggestions

Remembering Larry King
by secularethical
4,871 views

NATASHA MILLER THE GREAT
by cartermayes
19,930 views

Lawrence King: A message to lawmakers
by georgiaequality
10,484 views

Lawrence king
by Tanner92882
8,699 views

Dreams Deferred: The Sakia Gunn Film Project
by EamonnSimoneFilms
5,568 views

Lawrence King Tribute - Very Sad
by Trueling
26,851 views

This video is public.

Like | + Add to | Share | 28,034

Uploaded by cartermayes on Apr 18, 2008
tribute

149 likes, 1 dislikes

@dukiedu So will a liar or someone who kills people meet their maker?...Because no sin is greater than another...So who are you to say such...I am homosexual, And God still loves me..And i will see my maker, no matter what anyone says. Because God died for me, And though i may not be perfect, I will see him to thank him in the end...So i will pray for your sin for judging. ohcuddie 8 months ago 4

The thing is that gay people will never see their maker. Cause they all go straight to hell. dukiedu 1 year ago

@dukiedu Oh Really? When Jesus was on earth he never married, and He hung around 12 men and one prostitute ... The Gays are MORE like HIM than you would ever be! There aren't going to be too many "Bible thumping hypocrites like YOU in heaven .." hpcwsd 10 months ago 2

Recently confirmed Larry DIDNT die from a gunshot wound....he died from AIDS!! and Brandon just shot him to put him out of his misery..Also to put into consideration Larry wanted to give Brandon aids..but brandon didnt let him...instead he smoked him...Brandon did the right thing...Gay people need to stop spreading aids and get a life and stop being gay..when you go back to your maker are you gonna tell him ur gay?? and straight people need to stop defending larry... FREE BRANDON!!!!! uzumak1blast 1 year ago

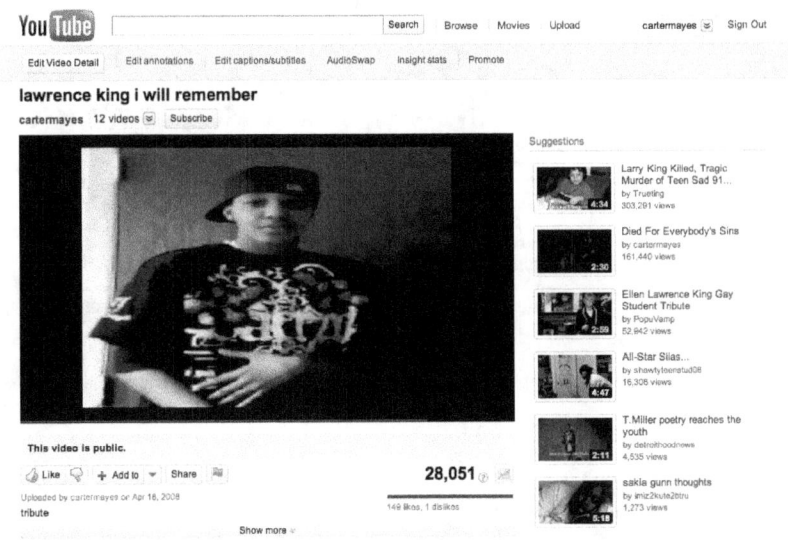

**lawrence king i will remember**

cartermayes  12 videos ⊠    Subscribe

Suggestions

Larry King Killed, Tragic
Murder of Teen Sad 91...
by Trueling
303,291 views
4:34

Died For Everybody's Sins
by cartermayes
161,440 views
2:30

Ellen Lawrence King Gay
Student Tribute
by PopuVamp
52,942 views
2:59

All-Star Silas...
by showtyteenstud08
16,306 views
4:47

T.Miller poetry reaches the
youth
by detroithoodnews
4,535 views
2:11

sakia gunn thoughts
by imiz2kute2thru
1,273 views
6:18

This video is public.

👍 Like  💬  + Add to ▾   Share  🔖                              28,051 ⊘ ⏄

Uploaded by cartermayes on Apr 18, 2008                149 likes, 1 dislikes
tribute

Show more ⌄

u cant just edit stuff out the bible because it doesnt meet ur needs @
frenchy4001..im not a evil person at all.i dnt even know tho the boy is that was
killed but i do feel bad for that kid. but as far as being gay..i rather be safe than
sorry DRKCOLORS 2 years ago

I do belive in god and thats y I say gays are going to hell because GOD said so
DRKCOLORS 2 years ago

Why cant love just be love...why does it have to have a title parisg155 2 years ago

I dont understand how gays can be bother straight people so much... how does
what we do affect anything straights do? i mean arent we able to love whomever
we want... and you say gays are going to hell.. but im sure everyone who says
things like that have done worse then love someone of the same sex. some
people act like we can actually help it. love has no boundaries and everyone
needs to see that.. ur amazing girl keep doin ur thang! crazihawiian1992 2
yearsago

gays are going to hell..plain and simple DRKCOLORS 2 years ago

*This has been flagged as spam*   hide
If u believe in god then u should believe in love and accept everyone the way
they are its sad to see that religion turn people like u into evil ....and if its what
religion does to people then im glad that I don't believe in godfrenchy4001 2 years
ago

49

TabNMoeShow

check this out                                                      11/29/07

hey... i dont know if you have heard of Westboro Baptist Church it is a
group whose public crusades against homosexuality have included
hate pickets across the country. The ADL report says that Phelps also
espouses anti-Semitism and racism, a fact that is largely obscured by
the church's highly charged attacks against homosexuals. They also
go across the country and picket dead soljers funrals with signs that
basicly say if the world didnt tolerate gay people these soljars
wouldnt be dead.... anyways i have formed a group on myspace i
would love it you would join your poem "died for everyone sins"
touched me and goes right along with what i am trying to stand for
anyway check us out http://www.myspace.com/godizluv5

Reply | Delete                        block user    mark as spam

50

**facebook**

## Heading out? Stay connected
Visit facebook.com on your mobile phone.

Get Facebook Mobile

## Sign Up
It's free and always will be.

First Name:

Last Name:

Your Email:

Re-enter Email:

New Password:

I am: Select Sex: ⬍

Birthday: Month: ⬍  Day: ⬍  Year: ⬍

Why do I need to provide this?

Sign Up

Create a Page for a celebrity, band or business.

English (US)  Español  Português (Brasil)  Français (France)  Deutsch  Italiano  العربية  हिन्दी  中文(简体)  日本語  »

51

## *"Today a lesbian told me that she don't mess with men AT ALL! There's a special place in hell for her kind!" Uncontrolled Storm*

Natasha's Inbox

**Natasha T. Miller**
**thats cowardly**                                    June 15, 2010

You erased me off of your friends list because I didn't agree with you. Well I hope that you find peace or a lesbian that still loves men. I pray for your ignorance and hope that you grow and learn the power of understanding, listening and accepting when you're wrong. Like yourself my brother is a black man so know that I love you and I pray for your survival. Goodbye old facebook friend.

Heads up, I'm sure you have lesbian friends and I'm sure that will offend them also so you might wanna delete before day break take care

**Uncontrolled Storm**                               June 15, 2010

What the fuck is wrong with you? Stop taking the stuff that I post so fucking serious, it was meant to be funny, its just a joke,...are you a lesbian? No bodies being ignorant. If you have a serious problem with what I say on fucking fb then keep that shit to yourself. If I gave a fuck what everybody else thought of what I post on fb then I couldn't speak my mind.

**Uncontrolled Storm**                               June 15, 2010

That's cowardly? Who the fuck asked you to even speak to me in anyway. Your beneath me bitch.

**Natasha T. Miller**                                June 15, 2010

You are so angry sir and for what reason? You don't think it was kinda cowardly to erase me because we disagreed? You're a grown ass man trying to build a living in something that requires a fan base, Ima need you to be a little less angry. If it was all fun and games I o fucking l. I'm not interested as much as I am concerned. I know you don't really think i care about a facebook relationship with you. I don't even know you so uh yea I don't give a shit about that. I'm just

52

a little surprised about your anger. You wrote a stat and I didn't feel it, that's apart of internet life. Now I'm going to wish you well and let you know that my facebook friendship will b here waiting when you want some honesty and forgiveness. I'm sure that asking you to not refer to me as a bitch would b asking for too much but please don't. Thank you

**Natasha T. Miller**                    June 15, 2010

Beneath you? Sir, I sure it you know nothing about me but If you'll sleep better thinking I'm beneath you, I'll let you, lol but know that I forgive you and these messages at 547 am are not for me but for you and the survival of a community. Think about it, I could've been your little sister and I'm sure you don't want men talking to your sister this way.

**Uncontrolled Storm**                    June 15, 2010

Something is serious wrong with you and you should seek help, take your opinion somewhere that matters. Stop taking what I post so serious, I got angry because you were trying to make it seem like I was just talking outta my ass and being ignorant. I post what's on my mind and what I go though in life, If I gave a fuck about peoples opinions on what I post then I would post shit @ all.

**Uncontrolled Storm**                    June 15, 2010

it's not that we had a disagreement, you just took the status that I posted and tired to make it look serious and me look stupid and plan ignorant. That's all,...I was just joking and talking my shit and you took offense to that because the had a strong opinion.

**Natasha T. Miller**                    June 15, 2010

I need help lol ok if that makes you feel better. I understand that you were playing but I'm seriously confused about why you got so angry?!! You can say whatever you want on your stats they're yours but I thought they were open to others opinions, the public. It's a Shame that this has been going on for an hour and A. You're still angry and B. You can't agree on the resolution to agree to disagree. You think I'm silly or crazy because I keep entertaining this situation but sir I assure you that it's only because of the bigger picture, take care.

**Natasha T. Miller**                    June 15, 2010

I was not trying to make you look ignorant in any way. I respect the opinion of
everyone but you have to understand that as a lesbian African American woman
In the entertainment industry I deal with and see so much hate from my own
community so it wouldn't b right if I didn't speak out wherever I feel my voice is
needed. I can take that it was a joke, hopefully we can call it a truce and move
forward.

**Uncontrolled Storm**                    June 15, 2010

See,...that status wasn't meant to have serious comments like that. If you knew
how I was on facebook then you would know that it's all real, blunt and meant in
fun from me. I'm sorry for being angry baby,...but it was a joke ok. Let's hope
nobody goes to hell,...lol!

**Natasha T. Miller**                    June 15, 2010

Lol ok I mean it's some people going to hell but damn we just wanna be
surprised when we or they get there. Hoping that it was all a lie. Ok good
morning I'm adding you back then falling asleep. You not that u have a semi
serious person on ur list and I know that I have an angry jokester on mine

**Uncontrolled Storm**                    June 15, 2010

Lol,...ok baby. Good morning to you too, I hate facebook beef,...lol!

Write a reply...

54

**Natasha T. Miller**
What are your thoughts on bishop Eddie longs investigation?

September 27, 2010 at 2:27pm via iPhone · Like ·comment

**Sherita Evans** Chickens coming home to roost...
September 27, 2010 at 2:35pm · Like

**Keshya Chett** if you admit to not being a perfect man... but your gonna fight ...this??? Nobody is perfect, but you gonna fight this??????
September 27, 2010 at 2:36pm · Like

**D Smit** I think he should be real with sexuality, if the charges are true. Let God be his judge. I don't personally care either way . I just wish he keep it real and don't live a lie.... what are your thoughts?
September 27, 2010 at 2:36pm · Like

**Keshya Chett** If you are not guilty, state THAT and let that be ALL. #dumby
September 27, 2010 at 2:37pm · Like

**Parson Log** To be that way if it is true and lead all those people and be a servant of god....would be pretty scantlous....but at the same time he is man....and man makes mistakes....in gods eye he is no different than me or you...sin is sin.
September 27, 2010 at 2:46pm · Like

**Ani Thigh** I heard something like federal and local authorities weren't going to investigate b/c it happened when they were 17 and 18? The legal age in Georgia to engage in sexual endeavors is 16. IF thats true, he's smart and knew exactly what he was doing.
But thats a community i'd be apart of or an advocate of. Thats a cult setting though, so unless he's really proven guilty, his constituents will remain.
PS: When some advocates that hard for Anti-Gay campaigns, I feel like there's an 80% chance they are hiding something and more than likely just don't want to out themselves.
September 27, 2010 at 2:50pm · Like · 2 people

**Iba Poet** he did it, the world is corrupt....now on with wat matters in my life....
September 27, 2010 at 2:50pm · Like · 1 person

**Macy Stuart** whatever it is, one should practice what they preach.
September 27, 2010 at 3:04pm · Like

**Kambry Forton** ...I'm just tired of these bible thumpers standing up there calling us good law abiding Atheists sinners and agents of Satan while they turn around and sodomize little boys. What ever happened to the days when people were proud to be pedophiles? I swear, I associate pedophilia with the church so much reading the bible feels like volunteering for ass rape.
September 27, 2010 at 4:26pm · Like

**MrsRockie Amenson** Follow Christ and not the man.... Everyone Falls short, it is just amazing how his cult follows him, not to mention there are more boys coming forward this wk, and the ones that have already came forward have been put out of there homes (homeless) and are receiving death threats!!! smh I pray for the victims... Never worship a man, Worship God
September 27, 2010 at 7:53pm · Like

**MrsRockie Amenson** and @Parson Not every leader is lead by Christ... The bible speaks of false prophets
September 27, 2010 at 7:55pm · Like

**Rockie Amenson** I'm sick of these people worshiping this man like he is a God! He has all these fools brainwashed! Now, he got his peeps treatening these boys life... What's really going on?
September 27, 2010 at 8:28pm · Like

**Kambry Forton** ...the whole CHURCH organization has these fools brainwashed. How many people actually read and analyze the Bible on their own? Even then, how many understand it? When they're done with that, which other religious texts do you read? You have to compare and contrast them with each other in the same way you do when you're shopping for good bargains.
September 27, 2010 at 8:31pm · Like · 2 people

**Rockie Amenson** If you don't read the Bible for yourself and develop a personal relationship with God for yourself, anyone can tell you anything. "I don't trust anyone research but my own!"
September 27, 2010 at 8:38pm · Like

**Tanya Tay'a** wow im readn this an everybody has a right 2 their own opinion but what if it was ur child or otha family member being touchd how would u feel no matter how lng it took them 2 cum 4ward it was wrng of him 2 touch them if he did . only god an the people nvolved knows da truth so GOD will handle him ...
September 28, 2010 at 4:34pm · Like

Write a comment...

## New message

To | Enter a friend's name or email address

Message |
CHAPTER4
Education is not the backbone of our society, education is
what we want to be the backbone of our society but
Entertainment, at this moment, is our spine. While it is true
that one can learn from entertainment, it is unfortunate that
mostly, in this day and age, one has to be entertained in order
to learn and often we can not tell when something is suppose
to be teaching us or only entertaining us. Celebrities, the
internet, music, reality T.V, plays, and movies are all great
things to have access to, when one has their own identity and
other sources of education but they can also be dangerous
things to have access to, when one has nothing else to be
educated by.

**Send**   Cancel

**YoungPhenom** *The new dougie dance is SOOOOOOOOOOOOOOOOO GAY lol JD looked like he was at pride weekend doin that dance. He 82 years old. 3:36 PM Aug 13th via web*

**tmillerpoetry** natasha miller @YoungPhenom and once again I question what's the correlation drawn between homosexuality and dancing?

**YoungPhenom** @tmillerpoetry many gay men I have seen dance, dance like a woman. So it looks like a dance gay men would do, but thats just to ME. Others may not think it does. but I already know ur going to say that GAY is not a DANCE, its a sexuality. So I'm sorry T, it looks like a dance for women. 1,281,725,468,000.00 via web

**tmillerpoetry** natasha miller @YoungPhenom but if it looks like a dance for women, what does that have to do with gay?

**tmillerpoetry** natasha miller @YoungPhenom what constitutes as a feminine dance? i thought dancing was art not sexuality 3:50 PM Aug 13th via web in reply to YoungPhenom

**YoungPhenom** @tmillerpoetry because it looked like a very feminine dance, and he's a man, and so it looked like a gay man would do the dance because... 3:48 PM Aug 13th via web in reply to tmillerpoetry

**YoungPhenom** @tmillerpoetry in 22 years of living, I've seen women and men dance totally different (in most cases) so I know what a woman dancing.... 3:52 PM Aug 13th via web in reply to tmillerpoetry

61

**YoungPhenom** @tmillerpoetry in contrast to a man dancing looks like. There are exceptions but in what I have seen, there is a big difference...3:53 PM Aug 13th via web in reply to tmillerpoetry

**YoungPhenom** @tmillerpoetry unless the man i saw dancing was gay, (not ALL gay men dance like the women I've seen dance.) but i've seen them dance like 3:54 PM Aug 13th via web in reply to tmillerpoetry

**YoungPhenom** @tmillerpoetry women. So therefore I draw a correlation and make a opinion based on that correlation. 3:55 PM Aug 13th via web in reply to tmillerpoetry

**YoungPhenom** @tmillerpoetry so not to say dancing is not an art, and that dancing is split into two types, but based off of what I've seen, it could.... 3:55 PM Aug 13th via web in reply to tmillerpoetry

**YoungPhenom** @tmillerpoetry an observation and gathered info over time from this observation and making statement based off of that info. 3:56 PM Aug 13th via web in reply to tmillerpoetry

**tmillerpoetry** natasha miller @YoungPhenom how does the way a man dance make him look gay? you argue that it can make him look like a female but how does it make him look 3:59 PM Aug 13th via web in reply to YoungPhenom

**tmillerpoetry** natasha miller @YoungPhenom like a man that sleeps with other men or love other men in a intimate way? 3:59 PM Aug 13th via web in reply to YoungPhenom

I dun got myself sucked n2 another @YoungPhenom n @Tmillerpoetry friendly debate/discussion/clarification situation. Always making me think 3:59 PM Aug 13th via **tmillerpoetry** natasha miller @YoungPhenom is art separated or defined by gender and sexual preference? 4:00 PM Aug 13th via web in reply to YoungPhenom

**YoungPhenom** @tmillerpoetry I'm sayin, I've seen a lot of gay men dance like women, not to say because they dance like women they are gay.... 4:01 PM Aug 13th via web in reply to tmillerpoetry

**YoungPhenom** @tmillerpoetry just sayin that I've seen this. So with me seein that OFTEN, if I see another man dance like that.... 4:02 PM Aug 13th via web in reply to tmillerpoetry

**YoungPhenom** @tmillerpoetry I dont automatically say he's gay, but the dance looks like dances I've seen gay men do. Not to say ALL GAY MEN.... 4:03 PM Aug 13th via web in reply to tmillerpoetry

**YoungPhenom** @tmillerpoetry just sayin that it favors some of the dances I've seen a lot of gay men do. 4:05 PM Aug 13th via web in reply to tmillerpoetry

at work passing time by debating with @youngphenom about the "gayness" of the dougie dance 4:06 PM Aug 13th via web

**YoungPhenom** @tmillerpoetry I believe in some way it can be separated but not defined. Separated because just like u have, Gay Clubs, Gay Pride u can... 4:07 PM Aug 13th via web

**YoungPhenom** @tmillerpoetry have gay art. Art done by gay people, with the gay cultures vibe inserted. And homosexuality has its own culture. So.... 4:07 PM Aug 13th via web in reply to tmillerpoetry

**YoungPhenom** @tmillerpoetry not to say that it can be defined by that, because a race or sexual preference can't define neone. But there are differences 4:08 PM Aug 13th via web

**YoungPhenom** @tmillerpoetry so there is no way I shoulda said the DANCE was gay, but I could say JD's dance moved favored, a lot of Gay Men's dance moves 4:13 PM Aug 13th via web

**YoungPhenom** @tmillerpoetry so if I go to a party and its a lot of gay people there, I could say it looks like a party that would go on at gay pride 4:13 PM Aug 13th via web

**YoungPhenom** @tmillerpoetry I wouldnt say its a gay party but it does look like one to me. 4:14 PM Aug 13th via web

**YoungPhenom** @tmillerpoetry but thats only based off my personal observation or past experiences. If it meows, I'm prolly gonna think it's a cat. 1,281,726,914,000.00 via web in

**tmillerpoetry** natasha miller @YoungPhenom There is no such thing as a GAY club, human beings are gay, not clubs. there is a building, with music and people that are in 4:17 PM Aug 13th via web
**tmillerpoetry** natasha miller @YoungPhenom the building are some clubs filled with more homosexual people than others yes, but there is no such thing as a gay club 4:17 PM Aug 13th via web
**tmillerpoetry** natasha miller @YoungPhenom similar to the reason there is no such thing as a gay dance, human beings are gay, not dances 4:18 PM Aug 13th via
**tmillerpoetry** natasha miller @YoungPhenom so have u ever thought about this: maybe if you see something that meows it's still not a cat. It's just something you've never s 4:26 PM Aug 13th via web
**tmillerpoetry** natasha miller @YoungPhenom een meow but theres plenty of cat like whatever it is somewhere just like it? 4:26 PM Aug 13th via web

**tmillerpoetry** natasha miller @YoungPhenom and considering you dont know what it is u probably shouldnt assume its a cat 4:29 PM Aug 13th via web

**YoungPhenom** @tmillerpoetry i know that all cats don't meow but I've seen a lotta cats meowing, so I won't say its a cat, but if I guess it was a cat... 1,281,726,943,000.00 via web

**YoungPhenom** @tmillerpoetry i dont think I would be wrong for my guess. It might not be the right guess, but are we ever 100 percent correct? 1,281,726,970,000.00 via web
**YoungPhenom** @tmillerpoetry so not enabling myself to say things are gay, but just making statements based off of previous experiences. 1,281,727,018,000.00 via web
**YoungPhenom** @tmillerpoetry okay, a club that has a night, that is thrown FOR people who are gay. A veggie pizza isn't exclusive to people who don't... 1,281,727,174,000.00 via web

64

**YoungPhenom** @tmillerpoetry okay, a club that has a night, that's thrown FOR people who are gay. A veggie pizza isn't exclusive to people who don't...

**YoungPhenom** @tmillerpoetry eat meat, but a lot of vegetarians will eat veggie pizzas, so although its not a pizza only for vegetarians..... 4:20 PM Aug 13th via web

**YoungPhenom** @tmillerpoetry k scratch that last example i dont know where I was going wit that one but.... 4:23 PM Aug 13th via web

**YoungPhenom** @tmillerpoetry OKAY T-miller its not a GAY CLUB its a CLUB with a lot of GAY PEOPLE in there. I already admitted, that its wrong.... 4:24 PM Aug 13th via web

**YoungPhenom** @tmillerpoetry to call a dance gay. But is it fair to say that because I've seen a lot of gay men do this dance, that it looks kinda gay? 4:24 PM Aug 13th via web

**YoungPhenom** @tmillerpoetry if i go to a party and I see a lot of black people, and they are doing the hustle. ...... 4:25 PM Aug 13th via web

**YoungPhenom** @tmillerpoetry and then i go to another party and its a lot of black people doing the hustle and do that 89 more times..... 4:25 PM Aug 13th via

**YoungPhenom** @tmillerpoetry could it be safe to guess, (even if ur wrong) (its just an guess) that it is a black people party? 4:26 PM Aug 13th via web

**YoungPhenom** @tmillerpoetry thats why i said its not that I'm correct that its a cat, but me guessing that its a cat isnt a bad thing. Might be a.... 4:27 PM Aug 13th via web

**YoungPhenom** @tmillerpoetry wrong guess, but its not wrong for me to guess that based off of prior info and observations. Ima be like damn it aint a cat 4:28 PM Aug 13th via web

**YoungPhenom** @tmillerpoetry but for me to think it was a cat was a pretty good guess. 4:29 PM Aug 13th via web

**YoungPhenom** @tmillerpoetry most def could be something i've never seen and it could be a million of em out there. Bu thats the thing... 4:29 PM Aug 13th via

**YoungPhenom** @tmillerpoetry if i've rarely or never seen this meowing thing, but I always see cats meowing, its an educated guess that it MOST LIKELY is 4:30 PM Aug 13th via web

**YoungPhenom** @tmillerpoetry a cat, once I find out that it is not a cat, next time I see something meowing I may not ASSUME that its a cat.... 4:30 PM Aug 13th via web

**YoungPhenom** @tmillerpoetry but I will still say, it looks like a cat, but it might not be. 4:31 PM Aug 13th via web

**YoungPhenom** @tmillerpoetry but thats in a perfect world. U know im not a basketball player, but if u saw me in uniform n the pistons bench..... 1,281,727,950,000.00 via web

**YoungPhenom** @tmillerpoetry u could prolly assume that either I like losing or I play basketball. Both would be reasonable assumptions.

**YoungPhenom** @tmillerpoetry you could be wrong it could be halloween and I snuck on to the bench, BUT, it would still be a good assumption that
**YoungPhenom** @tmillerpoetry I play basketball for the pistons. 4:33 PM Aug 13th via web
**YoungPhenom** @tmillerpoetry why? Because in the past if u saw someone in a uniform on the
pistons bench, you figured they played for the pistons. 4:34 PM Aug 13th via web

**YoungPhenom** @tmillerpoetry humans take prior experiences and knowledge acquired from everyday observations and they make educated assumptions. 4:34 PM Aug 13th via web

**tmillerpoetry** natasha miller @YoungPhenom because i assume you don't care about his sexuality as much as you just want

**tmillerpoetry** natasha miller @YoungPhenom so whats ur intent to harmlessly share with the world your observation of jd being a homosexual because he dances gay? 4:34 PM Aug 13th via web

**YoungPhenom** @tmillerpoetry we're all wrong at some point in the day. So if you make an educated guess based off pass experiences u may not be right, 4:35 PM Aug 13th via web

**YoungPhenom** @tmillerpoetry but ure doing a natural human reaction to experience. And u change once ur experiences vary. 4:36 PM Aug 13th via web
**YoungPhenom** @tmillerpoetry he could very well possibly be gay based off of the dances I've seen gay men do in the
**YoungPhenom** @tmillerpoetry not saying that he IS, and not that he dances GAY, he dances like a lot of GAY MEN i've seen dance. So Im saying... 4:36 PM Aug 13th via web

**tmillerpoetry** natasha miller @YoungPhenom ive never heard of a person saying "such n such dances like such n such, thats straight as hell" so i guess now im ?ing intent 4:39 PM Aug 13th via web

**tmillerpoetry** natasha miller @YoungPhenom so did u want to tell the world that he's a homosexual before he did? 4:40 PM Aug 13th via web

**YoungPhenom** @tmillerpoetry I never said JD was GAY. i don't care if JD was fucking A mermaid from Ethiopia, but yea, it was me wanting to share my 4:40 PM Aug 13th via web

**YoungPhenom** @tmillerpoetry observation. But its not an observation of his sexuality, just about how he does his dance. 4:40 PM Aug 13th via web

**tmillerpoetry** natasha miller @YoungPhenom there's no such thing as a heterosexual dance right? 4:41 PM Aug 13th via web

**YoungPhenom** @tmillerpoetry and I've never heard someone say this chicken is DESK as hell, but some1 mite say desk in place of good. Don't mean they ... 4:41 PM Aug 13th via web

**YoungPhenom** @tmillerpoetry had any side/bad intentions for the naming of the chicken's taste,
just thats who they describe the chicken. 4:42 PM Aug 13th via web

**tmillerpoetry** natasha miller @YoungPhenom you've seen men dance like their gay so i assume you've seen men dance like their straight 4:42 PM Aug 13th via web

**YoungPhenom** @tmillerpoetry idk im not homosexual there could be a homosexual dance. There are homosexual rainbow buttons, but buttons are homosexual 4:43 PM Aug 13th via web

**YoungPhenom** @tmillerpoetry yes 4:43 PM Aug 13th via web
**YoungPhenom** @tmillerpoetry and its not so much about men dancing gay or str8, it just looks like gay or str8 when they do the dance. 4:44 PM Aug 13th via web

**tmillerpoetry** natasha miller @youngphenom a rainbow is a rainbow. there is no such thing as a rainbow homosexual button. i've seen plenty of heterosexual people wear lots of rainbow 4:45 PM Aug 13th via web

**tmillerpoetry** natasha miller @YoungPhenom items 4:46 PM Aug 13th via web
@YoungPhenom seven colors that normally appears in the sky after it rains has nothing to do hetero or homosexuality 4:47 PM Aug 13th via web

**YoungPhenom** @tmillerpoetry is there a problem with sayn sumthns gay, or the reason ure saying something is gay? 4:47 PM Aug 13th via web

**tmillerpoetry** natasha miller @YoungPhenom so you make statements about the sexual preference of others out of boredom?

**YoungPhenom** @tmillerpoetry thats what im sayin!! I'm not sayin that its a GAY BUTTON, but if some gay people themselves claim it as that...
1,281,728,988,000.00 via web

68

**YoungPhenom** @tmillerpoetry im supposed to just be like don't listen to what nobody says just assume that its a button and it has no meaning? 1,281,729,035,000.00 via web

**YoungPhenom** @tmillerpoetry asian people do hip hop now, it wasn't in asia first it originated here, but i don't be like its a usa thing, i just say.... 1,281,729,102,000.00 via web

**YoungPhenom** @tmillerpoetry it was a art form that was founded by people n the USA but every1 can use it. But I correlate it with people in the USA 1st 1,281,729,170,000.00 via web

**YoungPhenom** @tmillerpoetry because this matter is not something I'm very involved in I'm not looking at it from a for/against side, just the basic .... 1,281,729,260,000.00 via web

**tmillerpoetry** natasha miller @YoungPhenom and you compare it to you making a statement about something as meaningless as the taste of chicken? 4:50 PM Aug 13th via web

**YoungPhenom** @tmillerpoetry foundation of the idea. If i come up with a name for chicken , thats what I call chicken, Not to say im dissin chicken at ALL 4:55 PM Aug 13th via web

**YoungPhenom** @tmillerpoetry but if I call it sumthn else its nothin wrong wit that. So now me comparing it to chicken is a personal matter. 4:56 PM Aug 13th via web

**YoungPhenom** @tmillerpoetry u feel as if its an 2 important topic to compare to chicken. Because you have personal ties, so when I say something out 4:56 PM Aug 13th via web

**YoungPhenom** @tmillerpoetry of no harm intended you feel as if it is a shot or a wrong depiction of Homosexuality and its not. 4:57 PM Aug 13th via web in reply to

**YoungPhenom** @tmillerpoetry whether I know it or not, it may effect society or you, or the people down the street. But at the end of the day... 4:57 PM Aug 13th via

**YoungPhenom** @tmillerpoetry whether I know it or not, it may effect society or you, or the people down the street. But at the end of the day... 4:57 PM Aug 13th via web

**YoungPhenom** @tmillerpoetry everybody has their own way of naming or labeling things. U label me a nigga before but Im not a nigga 4:58 PM Aug 13th via web

69

**YoungPhenom** @tmillerpoetry but I don't think (other than sumtimes) u think im an ignorant person. But you still call me nigga. Not out of harm... 4:58 PM Aug 13th

**YoungPhenom** @tmillerpoetry but out of u happened to call me that. 4:59 PM Aug 13th via web

**tmillerpoetry** natasha miller @YoungPhenom you don't wear fitted caps because you're black, you wear them because they're fashionable 4:59 PM Aug 13th via web

**YoungPhenom** @tmillerpoetry also just like callin women bitches, they aint female dogs, but we call em bitches sometime. Not out of malice but out of 4:59 PM Aug 13th via web

**YoungPhenom** @tmillerpoetry previous experiences. So is it me sayn Jd's dance looked like a dance gay men do, or is it me not being gay.... 5:00 PM Aug 13th via web
but homosexuals didn't found rainbows 5:00 PM Aug 13th via web

**tmillerpoetry** natasha miller @YoungPhenom no, if you have reasoning for wanting to know what the button means, you ask. you don't assume anything about other people 5:00 PM Aug 13th via web in reply to YoungPhenom

**YoungPhenom** @tmillerpoetry so im not at as conscious of the "wrong" that is in that statement. its wrong to call the dance gay, but is it wrong 5:01 PM Aug 13th via web
**YoungPhenom** @tmillerpoetry to say that it looks like a dance that i've seen gay men do? 5:01 PM Aug 13th via

**YoungPhenom** @tmillerpoetry because if its wrong to say it looks like a dance i've seen gay men do, then ur saying I can't make observations and comment 5:01 PM Aug 13th via web

**tmillerpoetry** natasha miller @YoungPhenom you dont depend on inanimate objects to define a person's sexuality 5:02 PM Aug 13th via web

**YoungPhenom** @tmillerpoetry im just wonderin if I woulda said, Whitney Houston is looking skinny prolly cause of not eating. Would you have come on my 5:03 PM Aug 13th via web

**YoungPhenom** @tmillerpoetry *commented on my comment and said so just cause she skinny she gotta be not eating?" no you wouldn't have. 5:04 PM Aug 13th via web

**YoungPhenom** @tmillerpoetry so ur disagreement doesn't lie in me assuming something, its assuming something about GAY PEOPLE. But we assume all the time 5:04 PM Aug 13th via web

**YoungPhenom** @tmillerpoetry do I have to walk on eggshells everytime I have an assumption about things? 5:05 PM Aug 13th via web

**YoungPhenom** @tmillerpoetry i feel you not wanting people to mistake gayness for something bad or anything. But assumptions arent always out of... 5:05 PM Aug 13th via web

**YoungPhenom** @tmillerpoetry hate or dislike or even education, it could just be that people make assumptions and talk about it. 5:06 PM

**YoungPhenom** @tmillerpoetry like u said, we talk about people all the time, but its not that we're hating or not liking this person, just are observation 5:06 PM Aug 13th via web in

**YoungPhenom** @tmillerpoetry didn't say that it defines it, but if other people of that sexuality define themselves by it...other ppl get that idea. 5:07 PM Aug 13th via web

**YoungPhenom** @tmillerpoetry just because u don't define urself by it, other gay people do, so if enuff gay people sport the rainbow and define themselve 5:08 PM Aug 13th via web

71

**YoungPhenom** @tmillerpoetry s by it then SOME people are going to see that and say well rainbows are exclusively for gay people. but a lot of them sport rainbow buttons and t-shirts

**YoungPhenom** @tmillerpoetry not sayin that everyone wearing a rainbow button is gay, but if u google rainbow buttons,,,,, 5:11 PM Aug 13th via web

**YoungPhenom** @tmillerpoetry (The top hit is...Over the Rainbow Shop Gay Pride Buttons) 5:11 PM Aug 13th via web

**YoungPhenom** @tmillerpoetry the second top hit is, The Liberal Store - GLBT stickers, rainbow buttons, flags, magnets ... 5:11 PM Aug 13th via web

**YoungPhenom** @tmillerpoetry so obviously I'm not the only person who associates rainbow buttons with gay people. Is that such a bad association? 5:12 PM Aug 13th via web

**YoungPhenom** @tmillerpoetry I'm not sayin damn gay people taking all the rainbows! lol im just sayn due to observation rainbow buttons are very popular.. 5:13 PM Aug 13th via web

**YoungPhenom** @tmillerpoetry with homosexual pride. Just like an african continent medallion is associated with pride for africa. 5:14 PM Aug 13th via web

I CAN"T BELIEVE I AM ARGUING ABOUT A BUTTON!!!! lol me and T-miller be some debatin mf's lol

**tmillerpoetry** natasha miller @youngphenom is you said you thought whitney hou hadn't been eating bcus shes lost a lot of weight, i would understand that bcus 5:17 PM Aug 13th via web

**tmillerpoetry** natasha miller @YoungPhenom losing weight is a result of not eating 5:17 PM Aug 13th via web

**YoungPhenom** @tmillerpoetry due to what you have seen right? so i've seen a lot of gay men dance like JD was, then i said it because i've seen a large.. 5:18 PM Aug 13th via web

72

**YoungPhenom** @tmillerpoetry amount of gay men doing that dance. Not that i was right about my assumption but its not a farfetched assumption 5:18 PM Aug 13th via web

**YoungPhenom** @tmillerpoetry and if I said that whitney is skinny, most people would say cause she's on crack. not because they saw her or asked her. 5:19 PM Aug 13th via web

**YoungPhenom** @tmillerpoetry she didnt' say she does crack so none of us KNOW FOR SURE! but we've all said she's a crackhead b4 1,281,730,805,000.00 via web

**YoungPhenom** @tmillerpoetry not because we want to bring whitney down but we observed that she's skinny and we believe its cause she's on crack 1,281,730,832,000.00 via web

**YoungPhenom** @tmillerpoetry so from past experience if sumone I know is wearing a rainbow flag/button or watever they have been gay. Not sayn every1 is 1,281,730,889,000.00 via web

**YoungPhenom** @tmillerpoetry but from my past observations most people who sport rainbow shit are gay. Nothin wrong wit it, but they've been gay

**tmillerpoetry** natasha miller @YoungPhenom its a very lazy association 5:21 PM Aug 13th via web in reply to YoungPhenom

**tmillerpoetry** natasha miller @YoungPhenom correction you not we, i've never said that whitney was a crackhead and i've never said she was skinny bcus of crack or not 5:22 PM Aug 13th via web

**tmillerpoetry** natasha miller @YoungPhenom eating 5:22 PM Aug 13th via web

**YoungPhenom** @tmillerpoetry so am I really THAT wrong for making an assumption like that? Not an evil spiteful assumption, just an assumption. 5:22 PM Aug 13th via web

**YoungPhenom** @tmillerpoetry because I was arguing with you about homosexuality and buttons and whitney houston. So i respectfully agree to kinda agree 5:23 PM Aug 13th via web

**YoungPhenom** @tmillerpoetry okay T-miller poetry! u wanna get specific wit the word. Okay a LOT OF PEOPLE in my past observations have observed 5:24 PM Aug 13th via web

**YoungPhenom** @tmillerpoetry and made assumptions that whitney houston has been using the illegal drug CRACK 5:24 PM Aug 13th via web

So two girls walk in, (who I assume could have been lesbians because they kissed and were holding hands) and I felt like they knew I was  now I feel like a bigot thanx

**YoungPhenom** @Tmillerpoetry 5:32 PM Aug 13th via web

I never thought I could get that tired from debating, i feel like i been running track got damn!!!! 5:37 PM Aug 13th via web

**YoungPhenom** @tmillerpoetry naw naw naw t-miller, i feel like every gay person in the world right now is standing behind u sayn, FUCK PHENOM lol 5:39

**YoungPhenom** @tmillerpoetry n then all the people that love u who aren't even gay but would b for u, so who really are gay, are there too #FUCKPHENOM lol 5:41 PM Aug 13th via web facebook

Email
tmiller@tmillerpoetry.com
Password
••••••••
Login
Keep me logged in
Forgot your password?

**Heading out? Stay connected**
Visit facebook.com on your mobile phone.

Get Facebook Mobile

**Sign Up**
It's free and always will be.

First Name:

Last Name:

Your Email:

Re-enter Email:

New Password:

I am: Select Sex: ▾

Birthday: Month: ▾ Day: ▾ Year: ▾
Why do I need to provide this?

Sign Up

Create a Page for a celebrity, band or business.

English (US)  Español  Português (Brasil)  Français (France)  Deutsch  Italiano  العربية  हिन्दी  中文(简体)  日本語  »

75

**Natasha T. Miller**

"Taking Dick and Picking Cotton" Not the Same Struggles" a statement made by D.L. hughley, expressing his feeling towards the comparison of the gay struggle to civil rights. how do you feel about this statement and the comparison of the gay struggle to the civil rights struggle?

September 14, 2010 at 12:01pm · Like · comment

Ford likes this.

**Carrie Wilde** equality is equality, plain and simple. it's only when you start to delve deeper that you find incompatibilities or lack of comparisons. when women's suffrage was compare to the civil rights movement, i'm sure ppl had the same attitude as those who compare gay rights to civil rights. the point is that there are inalienable rights that belong to all of us. we all pursue happiness...

September 14, 2010 at 12:08pm · Like

**Shearton vall** I know he's a comedian, but I don't think the statement encompasses all aspects of either struggle

September 14, 2010 at 12:13pm · Like · 1 person

**Shelly Grated** Wow, I'm wondering how you feel about that statement. Its one thing to be gay in America, its another thing to be a Black Gay American. I make that statement because statistics, and being the smallest (race) population in the nation. The smallest in the US, makes up the largest population in the US prisons...racism is still alive and well unfortunately.

Any way–thanks for the stimulating status update.

September 14, 2010 at 12:14pm · Like

**Darren Brax** Blacks went through way worse struggles than gay people,being hosed down and attacked by vicious dogs or being sent to

jail,gunned down,houses and churches being bombed...gay people don't have to go through that,there is no comparison,but gay people do have rights and I feel they should fight for them,but their fight is not the same fight our race went through during the civil rights movement
September 14, 2010 at 12:25pm · Like · 1 person

**Michel Rags** wow this shit is ignorant lol I woulda never guessed that gay people had rights if Darren Brax woulda never said that. But he forgot to mention that just like black people they are refusing to give "gay people" their rights "lawfully". or how homosexuals are killed, harassed, and attacked daily because of the lifestyle they live. But naw naw NAWWW that don't sound nothin like the struggle of black people! lol it just has all the same qualities of that struggle. I think people who have a problem with homosexuality are people who are interested in it, and are trying to find a way to involve themselves in that lifestyle, but are afraid so they give anti homosexual comments that don't really have any backing to them just to involve themselves but with a "thats disgusting or thats nasty" front. But thats just my take on it.
September 14, 2010 at 12:46pm · Like

**Michel Rags** Oh and D.L. Hughley is not funny and funny that his first name is D.L lol
September 14, 2010 at 12:47pm · Like · 1 person

**Ashton Marks** Although gays struggle a great deal with society, it is by no means to be compared to the struggle with civil rights. There are no Straights Only signs. Gays are allowed to ride in the front, middle, or back of the bus. A gay man is more welcomed in Fernadale, Farmington, and Birmingham than a black man. Gays and brown ppl's struggles are similar, but not the same. Thousands of lives were lost to gain the right to read, write, and be offered equal opportunity. Gays may face some of these issues as an individual, but have yet to be publicly oppressed or outcast as a WHOLE. Brown ppl were shuned as a whole race and disgarded. The black man is labeled a crimminal and the black woman a burden before ppl know our sexuality. *But DL was wrong. His statement displays his ingnorance of the gay community. Gays are ppl, not ppl taking dick. If thats the case, what are heterosexual women doing? Much more than taking dick. And lesbians dont take dick at all. He should've put much more thought into that statement.
September 14, 2010 at 12:51pm · Like · 1 person

**Lasthia Teria** Tasha, you know I never get involved in these deep discussions because, I honestly think people like being ignorant, and won't change and don't care too. Being I have two degrees one being in history specializing in African American History, I decided to fit in some facts, no emotion on how I feel just cold facts.

1. Being gay was illegal and enforced in this country up into the 50's. Someone could report a person was gay true or not, and a trial would immense. Most people were convicted. I mean how do you prove your not gay? This practice still is enforced in the military. I think that's a big sign that says "no gays allowed"

2. gay marriage illegal. Did we all forget blacks were unable to marry, during the antebellum period. What about miscegenation laws(blacks were unable to marry anyone that wasn't black) those laws enforced up into the 70's

3. 20% of all hate crimes are gay related. Racial crimes went down in 2007, 3%. While gay related still rise.

4. 98' Florida judge said on record, before trying a case. "I didn't know it was illegal to beat up a homo"

5. new Orleans club set on fire killing 32 ppl. Lesbian club bombed, killing 7, Robert Gay bombs gay bar killing 6. Saying he hated his last name and what it meant. he was doing Gods work. Many church elders supported him. Do bombings sound familiar to anyone?

7. Los Angeles police beat a lesbian couple to death. Police beatings, ring a bell to anyone?

8. San Francisco political leader Harvey Milk, killed for being gay by his opponent Dan. Only given 7years. How many people see similarities yet?

9. Rebecca Wright and girlfriend Claudia. Shot to death in 2004. Killer said their open lesbianism made him angry

10. Matthew Sheppard beat, tied to a fence and tortured for 18 hours.

I could do this for days but, hopefully we get the point.
September 14, 2010 at 1:44pm · Like · 1 person

**Michel Rags** good muthafuckin job Lasthia!!!! lol
September 14, 2010 at 1:45pm · Like

**Lasthia Teria** You know what Michel, I could careless about people's opinion. Hate the gays, if you want. However, don't insult an argument by speaking with no validity.
September 14, 2010 at 1:52pm · Like

**Kambry Forton** I agree, they aren't the same, but there's a common enemy so I think it's best that both sides work together. The problem is that so many Blacks are still controlled by the misrepresentation of the Christian faith. Try being a Black Atheist in the World. It's bigger than America.
September 14, 2010 at 2:06pm · Like

**Lasthia Teria** Oh I forgot to add. Private colleges and universities can legally prohibit gay students and expel them. This is a practiced and enforced in this country.

Also in many states equal opportunity does not include gays. You can be fired LEGALLY or plain out not hired for being gay...

Okay okay I'm done.lol
September 14, 2010 at 2:08pm · Like

**Darren Brax**You can't compare what the black race has been through as a whole to what gay people go through as a community,they may have similarities but all gay people don't go through what those who are abused or killed go through,every man/woman of color had to go through racism it's not the same for gays period,here's a comparison...one man out a family of 6 turns into a fiend...can you compare that to a family of 6 who are all fiends...not at all...not the best comparison but you get the point
September 14, 2010 at 2:40pm · Like

**Michel Rags** No i don't think ANYBODY gets this point, because it doesn't make sense, I feel people when they roll hard for us as a race, but a struggle is a struggle. Its like damn fuck coming together as a people, we can barely come together with other people who struggle against the same

79

oppressor that has been killing both gay and black people for years. Your bible tells you to love everyone but then teaches you to discriminate against and outcast homosexuals. Calling someone "FAG" is just as bad as callin somebody "NIGGER". Being tied to a fence and tortured and then killed because you're gay is just as fucked up as being hung from a tree because you're black. Its all a struggle and a wrong doing, but because "you're not gay" its not as big of a deal to you. What if homosexuals started tying "str8" people to trees and attacking them and trying to make their life miserable? Then you'd be in an outrage. I'm sorry but that ignorant shit is for the birds, or just for people who aren't strong minded enough to look past the flaws in themselves and in society.
September 14, 2010 at 2:52pm · Like

**Darren Brax** Wht gay people go through is wrong,and have to fight for equality...true,but what we fought for and had to go through is on a whole different level,let's not forget what led up to the civil rights movement...slavery...stori es like what happened in rosewood,it's just not the same struggle at all,gay people don't have to worry about the whole community being lynched,whole families and neighborhoods were annihilated,and the struggle lasted of 400 years and we are still dealing with racism,your heart is in the right place but the fact of the matter is that they are two totally different struggles
September 14, 2010 at 2:59pm · Like · 1 person

**Daruis Genius Waleh** Haven't had a chance to read everyone's response so this is based solely on the stat question. The statement DL made was a bit much but he's a comedian & thats what he does & I'd be lying if I said I haven't heard similar statements in numerous cicrles. I've Always had issue with the comparison between the struggles however. They're two completely different issues entirely(apples/tomatoes), the only comparison that I can see is the HUMAN rights issue.People should have the right to live as they wish.
September 14, 2010 at 4:26pm · Like · 1 person

Write a comment...

80

**Shapree DeAnn Smith**

Hey,

I wanted to let you know that you have an amazing gift! I showed your youtube to one of my homophobic friends, I've been trying to help her see the "light" when it comes to all issues of homosexuality and have had no luck.. She really enjoyed your videos and it opened up a dialog about issues, she even wanted to know more about Sakia Gunn. Its crazy what you can do in just minutes, doing what you do best! She still has her ways, but me being apart of the community, its not about converting people, but educating them in hopes they will make the choice to not judge.. Thanks again!

**Natasha T. Miller**

Thank you for spreading the message, equality, hope and faith. My video, your views, our struggle. I hope she has a better understanding and I pray for the continuation of your education and spirit of love.

**Jessica**
My Friend Eki Sent This To Me... How Powerful Is She? Check Out
This Poem From Jackie Hill! ;

**MY LIFE AS A STUD by Jackie Hill OFFICIAL P4CM
POET**
www.youtube.com
MY LIFE AS A STUD by Jackie Hill OFFICIAL P4CM POET

**Natasha T. Miller** My thoughts on the video: nice spitting, nice writing, too
damn long lol and hypocritical. Finding Jesus will not allow me to lose myself. I
appreciate her testimony but every story is not the same. Some people are
homosexual because they choose to be, because they were born to be, because
they want to be; not because they don't love Jesus. There are some people that
love Jesus a lot if not more than the poet and has had Jesus in their life since the
beginning of their lives/process.
February 9 at 12:42am · Like · 1 person

**Natasha T. Miller** I understand why she changed; because she felt like it was
necessary but that shouldn't give you a pass to tell others that their life is sinful
or that the way that they choose to interpret the bible is wrong. Everyone has
the spiritual right to choose their relationship with Jesus and I believe that
happiness and love is the answer. I like being testified to, I like being educated
but I don't like being preached to. Finding God is not the three step guide to
leaving behind homosexuality.
February 9 at 12:46am · Like · 1 person

**Jessica** ... We all Have Our Views.. Thats All I can Say. Love You :)

February 9 at 12:47am · Like

**Natasha T. Miller** My problem with this video is not that she's giving praise but that her underlining message is making other people feel wrong but the fact that she found her beauty and calling is beautiful.

February 9 at 12:47am · Like

**Jessie Shae** my girlfriend took this poem too personally lol, i enjoyed it even tho i disagree with a lot of what she said. I can understand her feeling and experience because im very open minded. she did a great job.

February 9 at 12:50am · Like

**Jessica** –Tash– I dont think shes doing anything but Telling HER Story... the way it makes anyone of us feel has to do with self, shes just saying what happened to her and how she feels... its all so intresting to me, all of it.. the views of others, the testimony of others.. its all interesting..

Marvelous–– i agree, she did well.

February 9 at 12:54am · Like · 3 people

**Jessie Shae** I agree too lol ;-)

February 9 at 12:58am · Like

**Jessica** You Know Poets Better than i do.. :)

February 9 at 12:59am · Like

83

**Natasha T. Miller** Lol no boo boo, don't throw that one at me. She could've said all of those things without the rhythm or rhyme and I would still understand that she was trying to tell us what she did and further encourage and influence more people to do the same. Not only was she trying to encourage, she was providing the formula to do it.
February 9 at 1:03am · Like

**Jessie Shae** I think poets are passionate Natasha thats all, and I know you already know that so i'm preaching to the choir. I understand how you and my girlfriend and we all are right. Everyone's reality and experience is different. Unfortunately, we as human tend to think our experience is gospel and truth for all when its not. Which is why I said I enjoyed the poem because im opened mined and I can understand all side but I do disagree because I'm so gay.
February 9 at 1:05am · Like

**Jessie Shae** Basically she spoke for all instead of just for herself and I get that. It was still very well written but like tash said it was too damn long but i did enjoy it lmfao!
February 9 at 1:12am · Like

**Darren Brax** You can be gay,straight or not like either sex at all and love Jesus and praise God but that doesn't mean you're living life according to what God wants and says,something that can't be misinterpreted in the bible is what's wrong and right,the bible clearly states what's wrong and right and gives us guidelines to live by,I could be living in sin but loving the way I live even though most say I'm wrong,I feel that I'm right because I love what I do and I feel that its me and I won't change for anyone or sacrifice who I feel I am because people say I'm wrong...I'm not living for God in that situation I'm living for me which according to the bible is not the way to live,I think the woman was speaking from her heart and that's what matters,and everyone is entitled to their own opinion no matter how they came to those conclusions,I give her mad praise because not everyone can do what she did,I loved it
February 9 at 1:34am · Like · 2 people

**Krista Brax** I want to keep this short
Great poem
I don't believe anyone is born gay but I do respect those that make choices to be
with whomever makes them happy at the time.(and believe me its always at the
time)
In my case I once made that choice as the poet did
The bible clearly states that it is wrong and I take that as His word
When one truly loves God enough it will be less of self and more of Him
I don't think that she was preaching but most of the time when someone is
hearing something that goes against their beliefs it will sound like automatic
preaching in full effect
I think love is a beautiful thing and it can happen with anything or anyone we
choose to open up with..past all races..genders..and objects for some.
Last but not least, you may very well know who you are, but as big and powerful
as you feel you are about the "real you" when you open up to God and let Him
show you who He made you to be, you will see you were way off.
In all, you don't have to leave the lifestyle behind , get married and have a baby
like me, lol, but you should be able to admit to yourself that your choices in life
are just that until they line up with the word. If you believe in God then that
won't be too hard to do.
February 9 at 1:39am · Like · 2 people

**Jessica** Amen to Krista And Darren, there are things i Personally still struggle
with, but NO MATTER WHAT the BIBLE Will always be right, The Bible Is Not An
Error, We CANT Rewrite it. You Can Not Serve To Masters, Its Impossible to Fully
Love God And Be Ok With (your) Sin... However You Are Living, Whatever You Are
Doing, If You Think its Right, Then I Guess You'll Find Out, And YOU BETTER BE
RIGHT! :) The Bible Is GREAT Instruction From GoD! Its Not To Confuse Us, Its To
Help us, Obtain Life And Defeat Eternal Death! These Conversations Are Hard
For Me, Because Everyone Thinks Differently.. Im Trying to get better with
sharing my Beliefs and not worry about peoples feelings so much.
I appreciate all of these comments.. hopefully they keep coming.. Just Ask
Yourself A Question, When You Disagree With The Bible, Who Are You Truly
Hurting?

God Bless Everybody, And Strength For Our Struggles!
February 9 at 2:00am · Like · 2 people

85

**Krista Brax** those who mind don't matter and those who matter don't mind, great job expressing your view.;) God bless all and night night!!
February 9 at 2:08am · Like

**Lasthia Teria** Saw the video. I loved her delivery and her testimony. I mean I couldn't stop listening. I wasn't going to comment at first. But here we go. I mean no disrespect to anyone and I think EVERYONES VIEWS AND OPINIONS ARE VALID If I agree with them or not. However, I see alot of comments about knowledge and about the bible. God clearly states in the bible that Education is the Key to everything. I think it would only hinder his children not to get a full perspective on everyone's views. Not saying I am a scholar but I have been blessed to have a step father who is very versed in Religion. He is an active Christian and teaches at Wayne State University in Christian Theology and ancient religions and practices. I grew up learning so much about religion and feel strong to say I learn more and more everyday. However, I see alot of quotes and pieces from the bible being used in the arguemnts and opinions above. I just feel like if some scriptures are going to be used. Than ALL Scriptures should be used. For instance. The bible say's that it's okay to beat women, to get stoned, that only the chosen people will go to heaven. The bible also say's that women are second class, they have no rights, children have no rights, bible endorses slavery,no eating shellfish, no playing with sikin of a pig(football) no tattos or piercings, women keeping their hair covered, not wearing plaids, not doing anything on the seventh day, treating your body as a temple no artificial foods should enter your body. i.e sugars, alcohol.etc. NO round haricuts...i.e how all black men wear there hair now adays, Leviticus where it states that gay is wrong. It also states that marriage is only legal if a woman is a virgin. I just hate if we point the finger at one lifestyle lets point a finger at them all.

Peace and Blessings,
February 9 at 3:33am · Like · 1 person

**Jessica** Its not about pointing the finger thats whats some of you dont understand, i expected this video to get a reaction, and i knew there would be disagreements.. To: Lasthia I believe that you are talking alot about the old testament, But.... Who Am I...? Moving On.... To Whomever Else– at this point im exhausted and honestly Would Rather Not coutinue this "conversation"... we all think and live different, the relationship each one of us has with God Is Our own seperate Business.. I Will Say This, There Were Some Comments Made Else Where, That One Should Practice What They Preach and blah blah, which is very true, but please dont take me posting this video as me trying to change people, Preaching, or make people feel bad, this was something that i was interested in, and im talking to whoever... we all fall short of GODS will for us,or do something

we know we shouldnt and its none of our job to judge others in that area.. Whatever you believe in may God Bless You All, And FINALLY GOODNIGHT! Feel Free to Continue To talk to eachother about this video, but i can no longer talk about this particular video today. Take What You Take From That With Love.. Xo-JB
February 9 at 4:02am · Like · 2 people

**Krista Brax** No doubt that everyone that has commented loves the Lord. Homosexuality is always a touchy subject because it sometimes involves love and after all that is a blessing from God, so its right, right? Everyone is on their own path and we can have all the opinions in the world, share them, will still make mistakes in our life and we still only have to answer to Him in the end. We wont have our group of people that agree with us on earth to support us on that day, and as long as we are all comfortable with that then live however you want.
February 9 at 6:57am · Like · 2 people

**Darren Brax** I feel you are only speaking of the old testament as well, the new testament doesn't speak on things like that, what's wrong is wrong but we don't always know wrong from right,God gave us free will...the freedom to sin and find out what's wrong and right on our own(with His help of course) some people won't find out their shortcomings or sins they have unconsciously committed until Jesus Himself comes back...now this was about the video of the female poet who spoke about her testimony which is why "gay" was the topic,but it goes for everything that people do that is wrong but they still love to do,certain rapists love to rape people...its apart of who they feel they are...a lot of murderers are the same way and the same thing goes for some who cheat on their partners...and so on and so on "its just who they are"...if you don't have the faith and love for God to take His word and embody it then you will never see the error in your ways,that goes for me and every other human being, if it doesn't go hand in hand with the lifestyle we choose then we disagree with it or try to find reasons why the bible is fickle...but its your life so live it the way you see fit,we all have to answer to God and will soon find out the truth about it all
February 9 at 7:29am · Like · 2 people

**Perry Millieon** I appreciate the showmanship, but its testimonials like this that perpetuate the theory that sexuality is a choice for EVERYONE. Life in general is a struggle and most homosexuals have battled their sexuality. I know I have, but it comes down to you are who you are. If you're going to live your life according

87

to a book, then you need to follow it to the letter and not just when/how it suites you that day.

**David Warrens** wow Im loving it Im a little late but first of all I must say Praise be to God on this conversation Even though we all have our opinions, we are discussing the Lord and His Word which is always good in His eyes Long as we keep it civil (which I see we are)

Krista and Darren you guys know I had to comment

Anyways the vid was great She gave a testimony Whether you look at it like she was judging or not she felt what she felt needed to been said I do not think it was directed towards anyone but more or less telling her story and also telling it to those who may feel how she feels but do not know if they have the strength to give that lifestyle up She is to some the voice they want to speak and cry out but can't or don't know how

Homosexuality according to the Word of God is wrong Now whether you believe in the Word of God or not is up to you Am I judging? No that is not my place or anyone's place for that matter Our job and only job on this earth is to love one another even those who sin Jesus loved us so much He died for us regardless of how wretched and unrighteous we were and still are today Our lifestyles should be based on the way Jesus walked No we can't do it exactly but we can try And the basis of Jesus lifestyle was love We are to love one another whether you are a murderer homosexual pedophile whatever the case may be Now that may be extreme but we sometimes forget the power of love and how it can change a person's lifestyle What upsets me a lot of times though is how some homosexuals pronounce their love for God but are not willing to make a change in the way they are living I have some habits that I am not comfortable with or better yet do not conform to the Word of God but I am doing things in my daily living to try and change them Do I follow the Word to a tee? No neither of us do and none of us will actually be able to It wasnt given to us to follow exactly to a tee It was given to tell us a story To tell us what God likes and doesnt like and try to live a life that adheres to His liking The Word then goes on to tell us the story of Jesus who was God in the flesh and to show us how to be pleasing to God and even then we fall short So Jesus died as a sacrifice for our sin because God knew we couldn't satisfy Him on this earth completely and that we WERE going to sin So once again why is the Word of God here? Not for our complete and total obedience Yes we are to try BUT the Word is here to show us a story of LOVE and how that LOVE is still here today and wants to be with each and everyone of us The homosexuals the rapists the murderers and those who find that Love are supposed to show it to those who need it

So to sum up, is homosexuality wrong. I follow the Word of God and the Word of God says it is Now is some of the things I do wrong? God knows they are But I know who my Father is and that He loves me regardless as well as the homosexuals All we can do is pray and hope that the love of God and His Word will show us the errors of our ways and will help us to try and fix them

Remember everyone, the Word is knowledge but wisdom is when we take the Word and apply it to our everyday living

God bless
February 9 at 12:55pm · Like · 1 person

**Natasha T. Miller** So is the old testament flawed or wrong and the new testament right? When the new new testament comes about will the new testament be considered wrong or flawed? I believe in Jesus Christ and I further believe the bible is full of truth and metaphors: metaphors that you have to apply to your life as an individual. "to sum it up, homosexuality is wrong" kinda sounds like judgement to me, kinda sounds like a contradiction of the message to me.

February 9 at 3:02pm · Like · 1 person

**Jessica** The Old testament Was "BC" Time, Meaning Before Christ ... Alot Of Things Were Changed Because Jesus Made Change For All Of Us Which Resulted In the New Testament... I Dont Believe There Will Be a New New, But We'll See, Just Like We Will See Whose Wrong And Who Was Right! Homosexuality Has Nothing to Do With Judging, But It Has Everything to do with the bible and what Gods Wants For Us... At The End Of The Day, Sin Is Sin, Wrong Is Wrong, And It Will Be Proven, Until then... Lets All Love Eachother through Our Different Views, And Be Kind.. xo
February 9 at 3:09pm · Like

**Natasha T. Miller** As for the video, that's not (for myself) a bible argument, it's an English argument. It's not just her giving a testimony, it's her trying to be persuasive and also passing judgment by saying what she was doing and what other people are still doing is wrong. I don't care how she feels about it, I care that it's being argued that she's not trying to convince others to feel the same way
February 9 at 3:14pm · Like

**Natasha T. Miller** Well Jesus is coming back again so after he departs will another bible be written and the first two, lost in translation or time?
February 9 at 3:15pm · Like

**Jessica** He Will Answer All Of Your Questions When He Returns, one way or another.. We Can All Agree That He Is In FACT Coming Back, And What Happens to Us When He Does, Has Nothing To Do With Anyone But Self. I Dont Know How Educated Any Of You Are about The Bible, but Its One Thing to Know The Bible, And Another To Know Certain scriptures. When You Want to know something about A friend, typically you go to that person, we all should do the same with jesus, when we want answers go where he is, where his word is, seek him, whether we believe or not is on us..

February 9 at 3:22pm · Like

**David Warrens** Natasha, I recently got into a discussion with a homosexual friend of mine And asked him if he felt homosexuality is wrong He said no I then commenced to ask him if he reads the Bible. He said no Hence the end of our conversation Ms Miller do you read the Bible? And Like I said before it is not a judging issue A testimony is her own personal story of how she has been changed You are your own person You can either listen to her words and want to change or not The way I look at it people are so quick to say somebody is judging them That is not always the case Now I will admit most christians do judge Is that right? No not at all As I said before that is not our place But we are called to testify and let it be known when we have felt the love of God pull on our hearts to make it change Her story may not be for you but it is definitely for someone

February 9 at 3:38pm · Like

**David Warrens** And as far as the Old Testament New Testament....The "rules or laws" back in the old testament given by God was acceptable back then The way peopled lived and the way things were done were different and those things that God asked of the people in those times pleased Him do those guidelines and laws necessarily pertain to this day and age? Some do and some dont I don't believe God gave us the old testament to follow all the way thru Once again we can't I believe the Old Testament was given 1. To show and talk about the coming of Jesus Christ and 2. Show us today how the people followed or disobeyed God They showed how people pleased or did not please the Father That guideline which is basically follow and do what God asks is the same principle for todays people The principle behind the laws we are to follow not necessarily the laws themselves Just like it says in the new testament The greatest commandment now that Jesus has come is to love God with all your heart and to love your neighbor When you do those things You are basically doing what God asks and is pleasing Him just like people in the old testament did with the laws He gave them

This is my opinion on the old testament new testament debate
February 9 at 4:02pm · Like

**Lasthia Teria** @jessica and Darren– Yes all of the laws that I stated above are from the Old Testament, when Jesus died for the sins of his followers. We were then not bound to the laws of the Old Testament. However the New Testament clearly states that we should observe those laws and know the history of Judaism since that is the father of Christianity. However, if we only want to talk about the New Testament. I can do that also. Jesus taught only two things. 1. Love one another. 2. Love God. That's it point blank period.
Secondly, It astonishes me that all other major religions i.e. Judaism and Islam actively teaches knowing their books. I.e. the Torah and the Koran. If you step into any Islam school or most temples Majority of the people can recite the Koran backwards and forwards in their ancient language. The same thing for The Torah. However, Christians as seen here. KNOW NOTHING about the Bible. We are a group of people who say's knowledge is key. However, we practice. "Do as I say don't ask any questions just believe me." The pastor or tradition is passed down but no one really knows what the Bible Say's, and if you ask any questions the conversation is always ended with silence. If we are going to argue the bible let's argue the bible. Not bits and pieces that we "think" we know.
February 9 at 5:21pm · Like · 1 person

**David Warrens** Ms Teria what does the Bible say that people on this conversation do not already know? I would like to be enlightened
February 9 at 6:08pm · Like

**Lasthia Teria** @David. I apologize but I haven't read ANY of your comments but you can believe when I get a chance I will. So unfortunately I don't know your

view on this conversation AT ALL. I have been at work all day and haven't been able to give my undivided attention to everyone. That is why I SPECIFICALLY directed comments to certain responses made, because I know I am not fully invested in what EVERYONE has said. My statements were directed to comments made prior to you entering the conversation. Distinctly about the Validity of the Old vs. New Testament. Jesus states in the New Testament that he came to fulfill the Laws of the Old Testament not destroy them. Scriptures placed in Thes and Cor both state that Jesus was avid in the following of Mosaic laws. So when it is insinuated that when I bring up laws from the Old Testament I am completely off the mark, I am confused. How could it even be questioned that the Old Testament is not valid for the Christian Faith. I completely disagree and think it is incomprehensible to even play with that idea. I understand as Christians it is believed once Jesus died for our sins that we were no longer bound to the laws but we are still supposed to observe them. Don't pick certain sins that our incomprehensible because they don't apply to your specific lifestyle. However, the sins that do apply to people's lifestyles that they choose to say things like "well that's the Old Testament" so there is no need to follow those words. Or "I am a sinner and growing also". As a Christian if you know your "LIVING IN SIN" then your living in sin. All in all if we are going to quote things from the Bible, know all parts and have scripture to back you up.
February 9 at 6:36pm · Like

**David Warrens** your points is true....check out my opinion on the old and new testemant debate that i posted on here when you get a chance and let me know what you think
February 9 at 6:39pm · Like

**Lasthia Teria** Most Definitely. I don't know alot but I know my bible.. And I know scripture extremely well..lol..Can't wait to read your comments Daniel ;)
February 9 at 6:48pm · Like

**Lasthia Teria** I have a feeling we won't agree. But I think I am going to more than respect what you have to say."This is what Makes God Happy"
February 9 at 6:49pm · Like

**Daniel Woods** Lol is it wrong that when u said u disagree, a smile came upon my face? I love to talk about the Lord It makes me able to see things from others perspective and maybe even learn something new So Ms Garcia if you find anything you disagree, please do share
February 9 at 7:01pm · Like

**Lasthia Teria** @David– probably because you definitely are a man of God. And you understand we are pleasing him. Nice to meet you Daniel. Excited to converse later.
February 9 at 7:07pm · Like

**David Warrens** The pleasure is all mine Ms.Teria Talk to you later
February 9 at 8:12pm · Like

Write a comment...

THE DRUMMER IN THE BAND AT THE ALL STAR GAME IS IRREGULARLY
QUEER... SMH, WHEN DID IT START BEING ACCEPTABLE TO PUT GAY
PEOPLE ON TELEVISION? FOR CHRIST SAKE GAYS ARE MUTANTS WHY
HAVEN'T THEY BEEN EXTERMINATED ALREADY? SHEEESH

February 20 at 8:28pm via Mobile Web · Like · Comment

👍 Tonita Msshay White-crosby likes this.

 Dog I swear I said the same shit
February 20 at 8:35pm · Like

 This nigga is Crazy
February 21 at 2:05am · Like

Write a comment...

94

**Natasha T. Miller**

It's always interesting and heartbreaking to see a homosexual agree with, laugh at or promote a homophopic Facebook status, Youtube video or tweet. Do you get on the internet without your pride?!

April 23 at 7:32pm · Like · Comment

👍 Complex'Distress Jackson, Dymond Jackson, E'toi Foreverthecheerleader Jackson and 15 others like this.

 **Fortunate Sonya** Yeah I agree that's weak.
April 23 at 7:35pm · Like

 **Tashi Cuntessa Acket** I feel that. Self hatred is the worst
April 23 at 9:04pm · Like

 **Da'Wana Miller** Y u gota cover up who u r! Like me 4 me or dnt like me @ ALL!!
April 24 at 2:10pm · Like

Write a comment...

**Natasha T. Miller**

"This hidden culture of men living a dangerous lie has ruined so many lives," Oprah says. "It's broken up families and put so many women at risk." How do you feel about men on the DL, why do you think there are so many men on the DL and do you think there are equally as many women but it goes undiscovered or fly under the radar because its dealing with women?

October 8, 2010 at 12:24pm · Like ·comment
Cheryl R and Shrita P like this.

**Chiantae Leon** I feel hypocritical about DL men because while I want them to be out in the open and honest, at the same time I want the right to my privacy, and not having to disclose my own sexual preferences. But if you are going to be dealing with someone, you take away their choice to choose freely, when you don't tell them about your involvements. It's one thing to keep your sexuality status a secret in general, but when it comes to sexual and romantic relationships you should be honest. It is messed up when a DL man moves between partners (male and female), and is not being honest, but the worst part is if they are not having safe sex. That is the most dangerous part. They hide because this society is rife with hatred and fear of homosexuality. They are afraid to be judged and rejected, like any other human being would. For a man, it is deemed especially foul and shameful to have homosexual tendencies. Only look at the way we teach young boys to be hypermasculine, call them punks or soft if they show emotion, and all so-called feminine attributes are considered negative for a man to display. We inhibit their ability to thrive in balance, to express themselves, to form their own identity independent of our limited sexual politics and gender role assignment. I think more women feel free to be lesbians or bi-sexuals because there is a double standard when it comes to how women are viewed versus homosexual/bi-sexual men. I'm not saying it makes it easier, but society has deemed it more acceptable, but that too comes with its own difficulties.
October 8, 2010 at 12:33pm · Unlike · 3 people

**Pandemonium Square** Just as many. Our culture has caused us to loose so many with Aides. Stereotypes, ignorance and sometimes we are our own worse enemies by bringing fuel to the fire. Respect is earned. Economic growth, education, pride in all that you do. Knowing who you are and excepting it. Love is for who you are not what someone wants to make you. Why be with a

woman when you're going thru more than with a man. So you hybernate until...
October 8, 2010 at 12:37pm · Like

**Mariah Urbanwoman Well** @ Ms. Chiantae well said!
I watched the Oprah show yesterday. Brought me to tears, because even though
I was angry with the DL men. I also understood why they were on the DL. I think
I more upset with the unprotected sex decisions they made, and for Ms. Briget
she had to pay for her husbands decision.
October 8, 2010 at 12:45pm · Like

**Tanya Tay'a** women should not b excused from being on da d.l just 4
da simple fact we want da same rights an jobs as a man but we want 2 b
excused from doing da same shit their doing now dats wrng . how would u like
it if u found out ur gay gurlfriend was on da d.l wit an nigga an she's claiming
she's str8t up gay ? do u know that there r alot of so called str8t gay women
who have came up pregnant oh wait what dat means FUCKN MEN WIT NO
CONDOMS we really gotta cum 2 reality on dis we wantd equal rights 4 women
so dn't act 1 sided when it cums 2 being on da d.l ... there also r alot of married
women livin on da d.l i have had friends ova the yrs date married women an I
have had married women approach me an u have gay women who say oh dats
just my sugar daddy what u need him 4 ? so eitha saran wrap it or put a condom
on it ur lifes worth more than a NUT..
October 8, 2010 at 12:53pm · Like · 2 people

**Chiantae Leon** I had a very painful experience with man I was in a
relationship with, who was bi-sexual when I was much younger. He was not
honest, and I found out his secret in the worst way. When I confronted him
about it he asked me if I had known the truth, would it have made a difference. I
was so hurt. I felt betrayed, and then too I was worried about his sexual
practices with me and the other dude (pre-op transexual). It was just one big
mess, and even though I still loved him I had to leave--- it just was not healthy.
What struck me is that he was in such anguish, I knew he loved me, but
obviously he loved the other man too. Back then I did not think about what an
awful situation that must have been for him, having his back against the wall,
feeling like he could not choose, loving two people, but not able to publicly be
with the other guy, and having to lie to me for fear I would reject him. Sadly, I
cannot say I would not have handled the situation differently. He lied, I needed
to dig to get to the truth for my safety and sanity. God knows how this story
would have ended had I not found out the truth. It's better this way, but now
when I see him I don't judge him so harshly. I don't think he will ever be open or

97

honest about his bi-sexuality, and I can't say I blame him, because personally that is such a huge risk and he would have to be real strong and brave, but he is not.
October 8, 2010 at 12:53pm · Like · 1 person

**Natasha T. Miller** Since its more acceptable for a woman to be open about bisexuality or homosexuality, should it be more shameful that women would be on the DL considering they might not face the same hardships as openly gay men?
October 8, 2010 at 12:57pm · Like

**Mariah Urbanwoman** Well I think its more acceptable for women. However in my opinion *from some of the bi women I know*
They have to put on a front.....a so what I'm Bi....I'm a freak, I do what I wanna do..I like both...I dare U to say sumthing.
That's them putting up a guard, because infact they haven't truly accepted their own feelings.

From what I've seen their are more DL homosexual women then Bisexual women.

I've been told by homosexual male and female friends...its more acceptable to be bi then to be gay for a woman.
October 8, 2010 at 1:10pm · Like · 1 person

**Chiantae Leon** Damnit, T. Miller, you are trying to unearth way too much today. LOL. Seriously, no one should have to be ashamed of their sexual choices or who they choose to be with. I think women fear the same things as men do. I think we want to mov...e in the straight world and be accepted there, just like men do. I think we face especial difficulty in not feeling dirty about sex period, with a man or woman. Many of us still want to be seen as feminine, and not castigated for wanting to be with or desiring a woman - because often times people act as if you negate your own womanhood by choosing to be with another woman - which is ridiculous. Or men feel threatened, and the first thing they think they can do is fuck you into submission, fuck you out of your desires- and it just does not work like that. And what about women - who don't ascribe to the whole feminine characteristics idea--- those that refer to themselves as butch or stud. The idea of being a woman is so defined through a masculine-patriarchal perspective - its difficult not to get trapped in the loop--- if you don't desire a man---then you must not be a real woman, and doesn't

98

every woman want a MAN? *snorting*

It's so crazy, and sometimes very confusing T. Women as lesbians and bi-sexuals is acceptable on such narrow and limited terms, that it still creates that marginalized "closeted" space we all keep running into. I can't knock a woman for keeping her sexual identity to herself, but I will say any woman worth her salt will be honest when it comes down to her partners and relationships. Everyone does not need to know, but the people you are involved with should know. It's not more shameful. it just means you're incredibly human as anyone else.
October 8, 2010 at 1:12pm · Like

**Mariah Urbanwoman Well** On CNN right now
7 arrested in anti-gay hate crimes in NYC
3 victims *men* were kidnapped & tortured and was raped with a baseball bat

This is a perfect example why people mainly men are on the DL

Just fucking Sad UGH
October 8, 2010 at 1:22pm · Like

**Natasha T. Miller** really, that is so sad!
October 8, 2010 at 1:27pm · Like

**Jesmin Culston** I dont care if men live on the DL, however if they are sleeping with women i feel that they should tell her that they sleep with men too.
October 8, 2010 at 2:50pm · Like · 1 person

**Amy Q. Pepper** Well i personaly was effected by it the guy that i was engaged to for a year and then the day after my college graduation told me he was bi and i had to end it. I really just wish people male or female would be honest and up front in the begining of a relationship maybe the person can handle it maybe not but give them the option
October 8, 2010 at 3:03pm · Like · 1 person

99

**Tanya Tay'a** i totally agree wit AIMIE give me da choice i have a right 2 know who im sleepn bhind cause ALOT OF MEN AN WOMEN ARE STILL NOT PRACTICING SAFE SEX !! u guys r excusing these men as if they stole candy from a store they r playn wit womens lives d.l is a wrd 4 a sorry ass excuse 4 a homosexual person 2 do it an get away wit it man or woman im sayn @least b honest wit the people u r sleepn wit they @least deserve dat much dn't u.. bi,gay or strait we all need 2 have safe sex an b honest wit our partners not da world cause da wrld can b cruel my lesbian daughter was beatn last by a security guard so i understand da dangers of coming out but im not excusing those who decieve an hurt othas.
October 8, 2010 at 3:41pm · Like

**Dave Grohll** It's a different generation...coming out is a relatively new concept.
October 9, 2010 at 10:09am · Like

Write a comment...

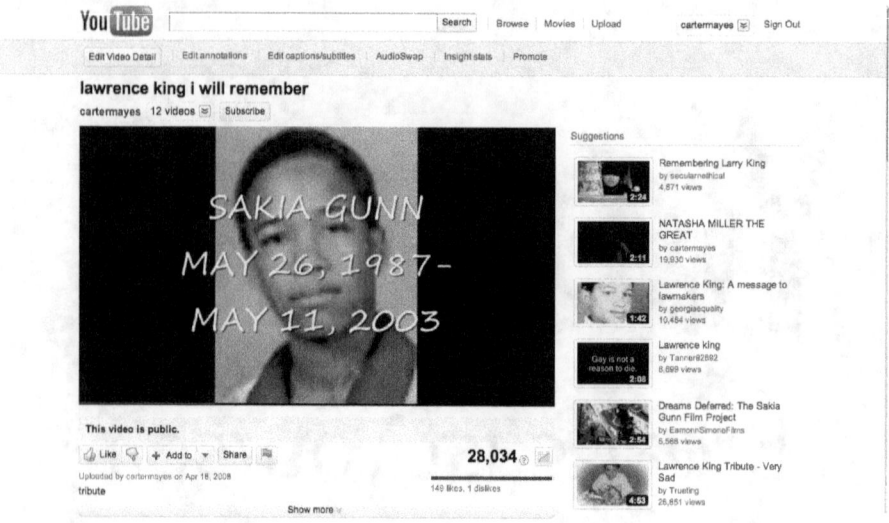

**lawrence king i will remember**

cartermayes 12 videos | Subscribe

SAKIA GUNN

MAY 26, 1987 –

MAY 11, 2003

Suggestions

Remembering Larry King
by secularnethical
4,871 views
2:24

NATASHA MILLER THE GREAT
by cartermayes
19,930 views
2:11

Lawrence King: A message to lawmakers
by georgiaequality
10,464 views
1:42

Lawrence king
by Tanner82692
8,099 views
2:08
Gay is not a reason to die.

Dreams Deferred: The Sakia Gunn Film Project
by EamonnSimoneFilms
5,568 views
2:54

Lawrence King Tribute - Very Sad
by Trueling
26,851 views
4:53

**This video is public.**

Like | + Add to | Share          28,034

Uploaded by cartermayes on Apr 18, 2008          149 likes, 1 dislikes
tribute

Show more

This is beautiful, this brought me to tears. I remember when Sakia died I was a senior in highschool, about 30 mins outside of Newark, and it really hit home. But instead of making me scared to be a lesbian teenager, it made me even stronger. I made a promise to myself to never live life in fear of what other peoples opinions were. I am proud of who I am because of Sakia. SHE DID NOT DIE IN VAIN .......R.I.P. SAKIA GUNN jerzeyluv23 1 year ago

"straight people are murderers!" fucking idiot etylers 1 year ago

UGH, this is so true. just because you don't understand it and don't like it, it does not make it wrong or a a reason kill... it simply shows the obvious fact that we are different... even in the way individuals choose to love. nikechick20 1 year ago

@matt guy your very ignorant how can you say that person had it coming.nobody has a death waiting to come just becuasse of their sexual preference. your a very ignorant person. chels471 1 year ago 2

*This comment has received too many negative votes*   hide
how can you jus sit here and feel sorry for these homosexual's. their deaths were tragic but they had the shit comin. mattcharger1 1 year ago

@mattcharger1 shit comin from straight murderers! philby74 1 year ago

I never knew how many people get killed just for being gay. You realy have to watch your back everyday and pray that you stay alive You fight everday to stay alive . Thanks for opeaning up my eyes to this. =) Military21Wife 1 year ago

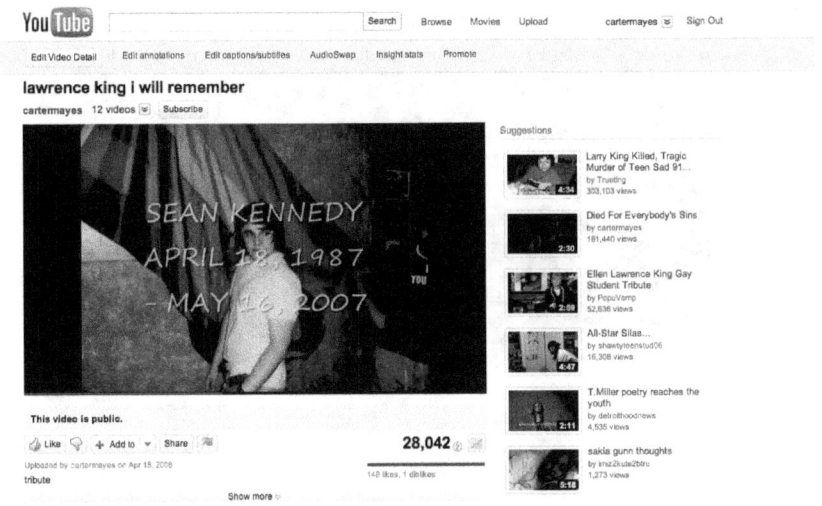

**lawrence king i will remember**

cartermayes 12 videos ⊻ Subscribe

SEAN KENNEDY
APRIL 12, 1987
- MAY 16, 2007

This video is public.

👍 Like 👎 + Add to ⊻ Share

28,042

Uploaded by cartermayes on Apr 18, 2008
tribute

148 likes, 1 dislikes

Show more ⌄

Suggestions

Larry King Killed, Tragic Murder of Teen Sad 91...
by Truefing
303,103 views

Died For Everybody's Sins
by cartermayes
181,440 views

Ellen Lawrence King Gay Student Tribute
by PepuVamp
52,836 views

All-Star Silas...
by shawtyteenstud06
16,308 views

T.Miller poetry reaches the youth
by detroithoodnews
4,535 views

sakla gunn thoughts
by irnz2ksde2btru
1,273 views

u knew what this was about why watch it?...don't talk bad about someone if u don't agree or got anything good to say don't say it....why keep watching it?....i hate when people do that!!!that's stupid...i wish it was a way for youtube to block ignorant people why get on sum gay shit if u don't like gay people?...dumb but that's america..still ignorant and afraid of what bc we're not like u look in the mirror there's only whatone of u! people like u make us all relate to ignorance and hate serita22 1 year ago

*This comment has received too many negative votes* hide
fuckin gay bitch motherfucker go die bitch lusti89 1 year ago

your stupid your fucken psycho you should die, who would care?? kaelinjohns 1year ago

*This comment has received too many negative votes* hide
fuck off mothercuekr u singin for a gay hahah bcoz he iz dead lol celebrate hiz death n for all oher gay ppl thoez died n pray for rest of them to die soon n u die toooomotherfuker go suck yr dad ballllz coz thatz all u gay motherfuckerz want a dick in the ass or in the mouth motherfucker animalz u ppl hav no ritez to b in thz world motherfuckerz lusti89 1 year ago

this crime that the boy committed is scary to me because my brother is gay.
mochababy2005 2 years ago

103

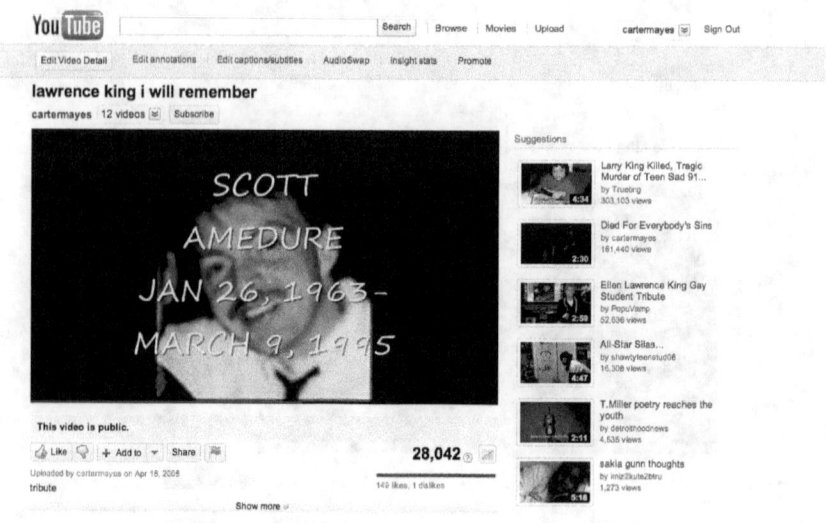

**lawrence king i will remember**

cartermayes   12 videos ⌄   Subscribe

SCOTT
AMEDURE
JAN 26, 1963 -
MARCH 9, 1995

Suggestions

Larry King Killed, Tragic Murder of Teen Sad 91...
by Truelorg
303,103 views   4:34

Died For Everybody's Sins
by cartermayes
161,440 views   2:30

Ellen Lawrence King Gay Student Tribute
by PopuVamp
52,636 views   2:59

All-Star Silas...
by shawtyteenstud06
16,308 views   4:47

T.Miller poetry reaches the youth
by detroithoodnews
4,535 views   2:11

sakia gunn thoughts
by imiz2kute2thru
1,273 views   5:18

This video is public.

👍 Like 👎   + Add to ⌄   Share 🚩      28,042 ⌄ ✎

Uploaded by cartermayes on Apr 18, 2008     149 likes, 1 dislikes
tribute

Show more ⌄

damn girl thats so true...no child deserves to be treated differently because of who they love..we as homosexuals dont attack str8 people because of how they are so WHY SHOULD WE BE TREATED DIFFERENTLY?this shit touched home for me"until they become victims of a system that teaches HETROSEXUALS to watch their backs because surprisingly they are the ones under attack,not us" that part rite there had me in TEARS i love this..   latipha08 2 years ago

wow that was so sad. Y do people have to kill others. Dont anybody know GOD created all, and for a person to take another persons life that pitiful
lakeshia85 2 years ago

Absolutely amazing, it truly is sad that we have to hide our love, or it could cost us our lives davida4156 2 years ago

You are a horrible homosexual, racist asshole who gets his kicks by dishing out this twisted little feelings ove the internet. You ARE a sad, sad little man.blainus1982 2 years ago 4

all those who mocks gay is wrong ask ur self does god ask you to hate, i have many gay friend and i dnt give a crap what they do. i know they're human being gay is not a choice is how you born. its said if u have an extra y chromosome to male/female. so why hate? its just make you look ugly make you look like a monster who hate those who r brave comming out. gay/bi r every lonely unlike you str8 they have to hide their feeling toward those they love. so plz dnt h8...ok?
xxAER0xx 2 years ago

104

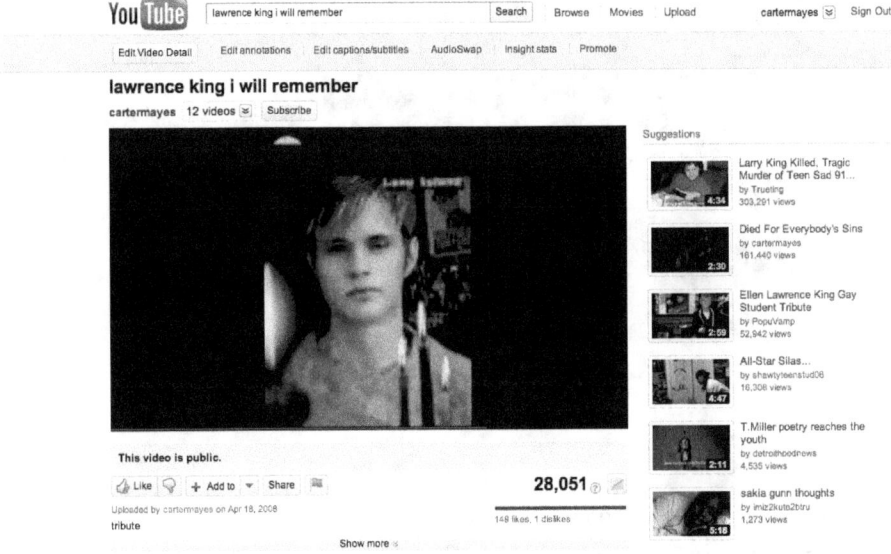

Thanks for the video memory for Lawrence Kings, thanks for the poem beautifully crafted, thanks for not forgetting others, I cant begin to fathom the extend of damage in my country Nigeria, if we cannot comprehend freedom for gay people in America. May the souls of the departed rest in peace, may justice roll down like spring water, may their blood fight for justice, may we live to witness change for equality in the universe. Rev Jide Macaulay, Lagos Nigeria. HouseOfRainbow 2 years ago

Lawrence King was one ugly baby TheBurgerKing787878 2 years ago

Why don't you stop hating on other people because your insecure about yourself staffwaterboy 2 years ago 2

Deep....Lord have Mercy...Bein a Lesbian..That is really scary...Once a point a time I would be hated or killed for being black..we sort of get past that...and nowI'm hated for being gay...That was nice..Touching... MissBenn25 2 years ago

Okay me and my best friend were watching your videos and came across this one. Personally I myself think that its fucking sick that EVERYONES making it such a big deal about our sexual orientation with being either

gay,lesbian,bisexual what ever... I dont see how or why someone would be so cruel to actually KILL someone over someone they love or want to be with in life. Its all bullshit to me. I'm gonna be with who i want regardless kill me if you want to. MiSSKEY1211 2 years ago

**lawrence king i will remember**
cartermayes   12 videos ⊌   Subscribe

SEAN KENNEDY
APRIL 18, 1987
– MAY 16, 2007

Suggestions

Larry King Killed, Tragic
Murder of Teen Sad 91...
by Trueling
303,103 views

Died For Everybody's Sins
by cartermayes
161,440 views

Ellen Lawrence King Gay
Student Tribute
by PopoVamp
52,636 views

All-Star Silas...
by shawtyteenstud06
16,308 views

T.Miller poetry reaches the
youth
by detroithoodnews
4,535 views

sakla gunn thoughts
by imi2kute2bru
1,273 views

This video is public.

👍 Like   👎   + Add to ▾   Share  

28,042

Uploaded by cartermayea on Apr 18, 2009

tribute

149 likes, 1 dislikes

Show more ⌄

it takes more of a man to admit hes gay, then it does for a biggot to hide behind an IP adress and call us down BrodeyBitch 2 years ago 2

your good fuck people ho thing we are wrong there mothers are wrong yes I am from the netherlands here we life in peace together peace out heaters merlien 2 years ago

You little 13 year old bitch, your username makes me wanna gag! Who the fuck would wanna remember a little homosexual mutant who came to school dressed in lipstick and skirts! Your as big of a faggot as cartermayes and Larry King pimpstatus201 2 years ago

your a faggot cartermayes pimpstatus201 2 years ago

Yo this was hot. And to all those Haters' out there. I laugh you off. You know they say the people who talks down about it are hiding it themselves. lol. This is ridiculous. A nation of oppression. When will people stop trying to bring everyone else down because of their insecurities. People need to wake up and realize it is the ones that you hate that determines your fate. Do not Judge, it is not your job. That does not make you better. RIP to all who have lost their lives to this stupidity Da1NonliAKA 2 years ago 2

it is sad that this happened, its show how close minded people really are, its a shame MiSSLiVEYRENEE08 2 years ago

106

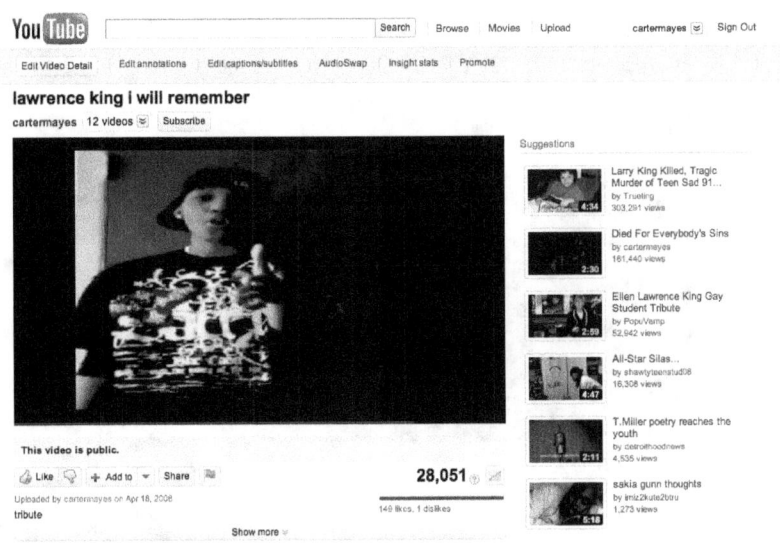

its gender expression that's like saying a jock shouldn't wear their letterman jacket to school BrodeyBitch 2 years ago

Some overplay it and do it just because they know it bothers some peopleI do feel bad for the pain that some people go through for being Gay. However some Gays overplay it and bring some of the issues they have on themselves. Bringing a purse to school or wearing a dress is just asking for trouble. I do think Gays should have some respect for strait people and understand that flamboyant behavior makes some uncomfortable. You can be Gay without be a flaming queer. billybassman21 2 years ago

*This comment has received too many negative votes*  hide
You might be used to hearing this, but YOUR A FAGGOT CARTERMAYES. You like to "remember" homosexual faggots? How bout you remember how this sick demented vile creature came to school everyday dressed like a transexual faggot and jacked off in the gym locker room jizzing all over the place as the boys were changing their clothes.. This animals deserved to die, and not just die the way he did.. he deserved to be tortured and mutilated and fucking burned at the stake for his sick disgusting acts FagMurderer666 2 years ago

dude go suck a cock u know u lov it stop hiding the fact u are gay we all know about guys like :) :) your fun slimboy102 2 years ago

You're just another faggot with a mental illness who needs to be shot. I hope you get a bullet in the back of your head when you and boyfriend are walking down the street holding hands you sick creature. FagMurderer666 2 years ago

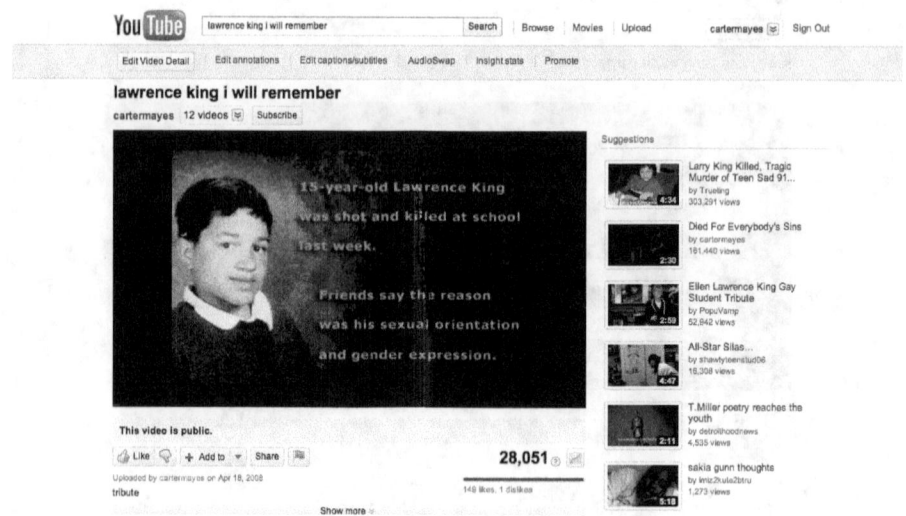

The faggot sexual harass Brandon, I do the same thing. Hope Lawrence queer resurrect, so can I kill him again. Burn in hell Larry queer! You in the vid, shut the fuck up! Thesniper2009 2 years ago

lol i agree. i feel bad for brandon, it's almost like hes being punished for doing somerhing good. 1 less fag in the world, the better. iRiShplayaa13 2 years ago

I don't think yourself and people like tupacsk8er hate us, I think that you need attention. this is a plea for someone to notice you and I do so are u happy now? You hate gays and now youtube knows about it! This is not about gay vs straight, it's about love vs hate and if you choose to hate and that's' a personal choice. I hope that God and time removes your blindness one day soon. cartermayes 2 years ago

are you a perfect sinner? you think because you are straight you're going to heaven?? you're so hateful, that God will judge your day..the whole world have sinned it's day of grace. ehouston 2 years ago 2

no kingston the ? is: what straight man spends his precious straight time looking for gay tributes to post hate comments. it must be really lonely in that closed minded world of yours. cartermayes 2 years ago

prison inmates will teach you homosexuality unfortuntely...keep hating and thats where you;ll be ..ehouston 2 years ago

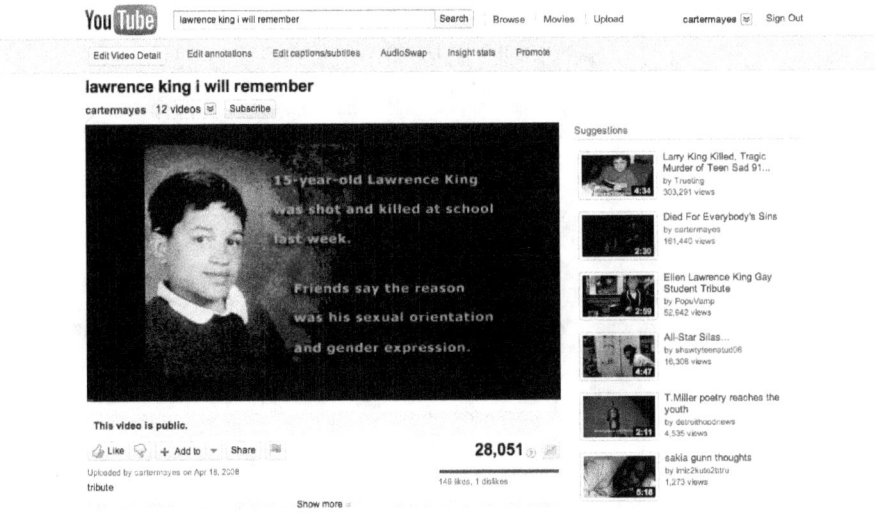

**lawrence king i will remember**
cartermayes  12 videos ⌄   Subscribe

15-year-old Lawrence King was shot and killed at school last week.

Friends say the reason was his sexual orientation and gender expression.

Suggestions

Larry King Killed. Tragic Murder of Teen Sad 91...
by Trueting
303,291 views

Died For Everybody's Sins
by cartermayes
161,440 views

Ellen Lawrence King Gay Student Tribute
by PopuVamp
52,642 views

All-Star Silas...
by showrytennstud06
16,306 views

T.Miller poetry reaches the youth
by detroithoodnews
4,535 views

sakia gunn thoughts
by lmic2kute2btru
1,273 views

**This video is public.**

👍 Like  👎  + Add to ⌄  Share 📧                      28,051

Uploaded by cartermayes on Apr 18, 2008
tribute                                          149 likes, 1 dislikes

Show more ⌄

yes i am a faggot, thank u for pointing that out. i had no idea i was until you just made that awesome discovery! without straight people like u pointing out all the gay people in the world, there sure would be no gay people in the world. people like u deserve a medal. ;) cartermayes 2 years ago

no cartermayes your fagot ass will be burning minotaro1 2 years ago

*This comment has received too many negative votes*   hide
No, he's not in heaven. He's gay so he's burning in hell!!!! lmao!!!!!!!! SiSenior333
2 years ago

wow watch this really touched me the most that touched me was when u said teens geting put out for coming out bc i just came out to all my family yesterday & my step dad told me to get out & half them hate me & the other half is like just in shock i think from me coming out & telling all them but i love how u did this & spoke the truth & all u should do alot more things like this ILoVeMyBaByBoY79 2 years ago 2

god is keeping lawrence king in heaven with him he is with the angels right now brothers Shreif1989 2 years ago 3

this is a great video i waz like larry's sister it so nice 2 see that you wud say that 4 evrii one 2 see and heer... babygurltj1234 2 years ago

Thank you for making such a bold statement against homophobia and racism. As a gay Iranian male it makes me feel good to know someone in the world has such a good heart. God bless you. liv4life1984 2 years ago

109

latipha08

knw you read alot but please read and reply                                      08/2:

i know you may have alot of these messages to read..but from poet to
poet..you touch me DEEPLY..i would make my own videos to try
touching kids and people deeply in need of someone to talk to but i
am a COLLAGE CHEERLEADER and will be descriminated against
if i do so.the way you use your words,the way you lower your voice or
bring to a booming high rise when needed is great.to be honest you
are one of the greatest out there..that one "america the great"
touched me deeply..and not to mention your "sucide" video that also
touched me deeply too because i most of my friends feel that way
towards them selves for being gay..which leades me to that
l"awrence king" vid..you did your damn thing..all props to you.i was
one of those teenagers that got put out for comming out so i feel that
pain keep making these videos referencing to any of these matters
because like you help me to get over certain stuff you have that effevt
on the younger ones....anyway im jay and i just had to tell you that
your words touch me deeply:]

Reply | Delete                                            block user | mark as spam

110

"Lawrence King, I Will Remember" **The poem from youtube**

A fearless fifteen-year-old little boy openly carrying a purse to school
Is more beautiful than asking your secret crush to watch "The Notebook"
With you
On Valentines Day
And more courageous than a American solider going to Iraq to bake cookies for al-
Qaida during the war
But they don't see it that way
We live in a today where gays are the new terrorist
 Females in baggy jeans are viewed as bomb wearing Arabic's
Armed and dangerous, ready to take over a nation full of insecurities
Those insecurely accusing us of starting a war against "straightcism"
This is where discrimination and racism rules the majority
And classroom authorities ignore death threats
Because middle school kids are all talk
Until chalkboards are covered in the brains and blood
Of Lawrence King
Spilled onto the California diversity bill
That will remember him but never bring him back
To maybe one day be an activist for gay rights
Be denied his rights to get married
Get thrown out of his high school prom for coming with a man
Receive a rejection letter from an adoption agency full of kids needing a home
But feel like a household with two fathers as lovers is wrong
So would rather have children, sit and wait on parents that may never come
Or just graduate from middle school
Lawrence king
I will remember you
Every time I'm not allowed over for dinner at my girlfriends parents house
Every time I hear about a kid getting put out for coming out
Sakia Gunn
Matthew Shepard
Scott Amedure
I will remember you
I've seen some of your stories talked about on national TV
But then disappear quickly
As if your tragedies shouldn't be broadcasted daily in this world full of hate crimes
I hate time like this
Where kids think it's all right to live and just be kids
But instead they become victims of system that teaches heterosexual to watch their
backs
Surprisingly they are viewed as being the ones under attack
Not us, that can't love according to out hearts,
Larry, you played your part

111

On February 12th, at 8:15 A.M, with your insides splattered across keyboardsAnd fellow students
You proved that what and how you love is worth dying for
And a deadly shooting, only releases your spirit
To live free from this judgmental globe
I hope your killers get what they deserve
But most importantly, I hope they one day know
Beyond prison lessons
That our love for the same sex is not for them to condemn
I hope life teaches them, that all people should be created equal
Even if you are not interested in the other kinds of math
Lawrence when you laugh
Shake a cloud, please
So I can believe that there's hope in the sky
For people like you and I
The ones who insist on being ourselves, no matter what consequences may follow
For us
Who swallow rainbows
And fill our stomachs with pride
Lawrence king, thank you for being brave enough to be yourself
We will always
Remember
You

Natasha Miller

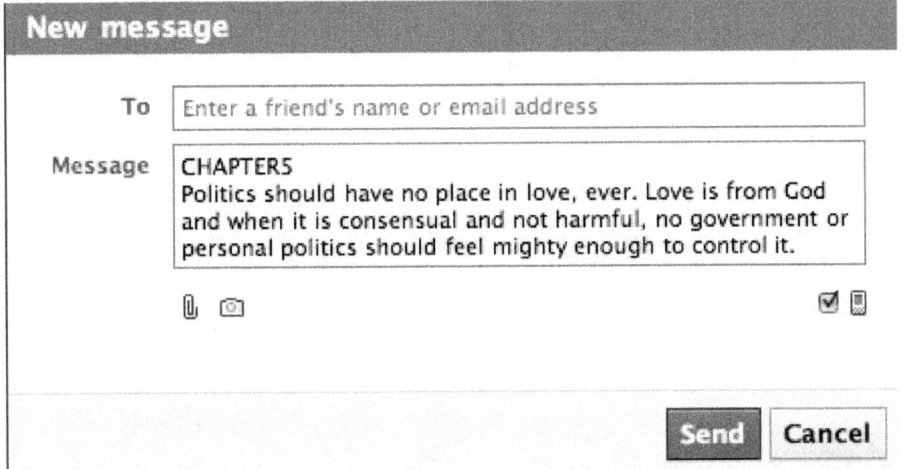

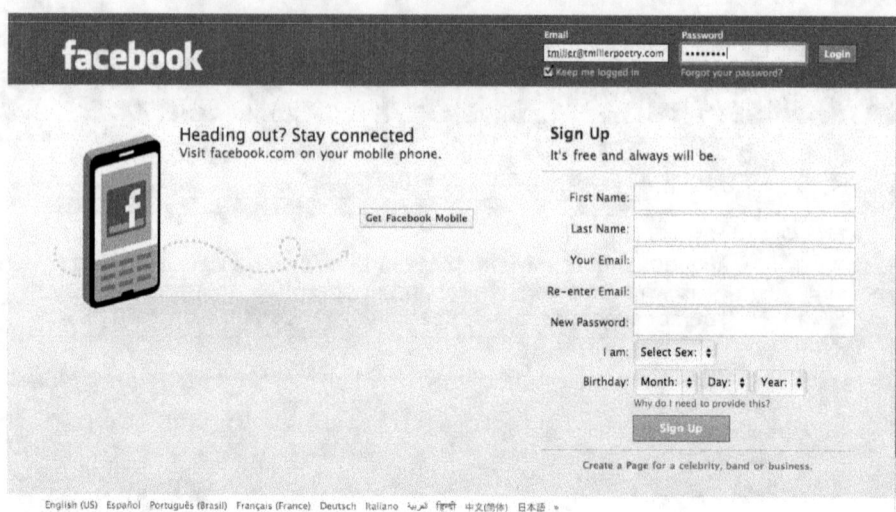

**Natasha T. Miller**

The anti-LGBT bill in Uganda has been stopped FOR NOW but the fight will go on FOREVER! Pray, then find a positive action to take

May 11 at 3:51pm · Like · Comment

👍 Complex'Distress Jackson, Erika Hudson-Mack, Renae Balentine and 7 others like this.

Write a comment...

**Natasha T. Miller**
As of Tuesday sept 21st, the legislation that would've repealed the law banning gays from serving in the military had been blocked:" Dear America, there's not a moment that gays are not fighting for life and freedom. These are the people you should want defending your country: the ones that fight daily for what they love; the ones who know what war is all about.

September 21, 2010 at 3:53pm via iPhone · Like ·comment
Leonard, Evans, Calvin and 27 others like this.

**Taylor Thompson** "the ones that know what war is all about." Wow.
September 21, 2010 at 4:02pm · Like

**Latosh Solmon** i just had to do a culture training for gays at my job but believe gays wont have a fight long trust me ur community is so big now
September 21, 2010 at 4:04pm · Like

**Darren Brax** They have to keep it to themselves when they serve in the military, and I really don't understand this, what does a persons sexual preference have to do with them serving in the military and fighting for their country, and what happens to a homosexual when the military finds out they are gay...do they kick them out or send them to jail...or what about if they already fought for their country and have been awarded medals for their bravery...do they take the awards away...saying "this isn't fair" would be singing the same ol' song, something needs to change
September 21, 2010 at 4:16pm · Like · 2 people

**Jesmin Culston** Maybe Im a lil too left field, and even more liberal than the average person, but why do people have to be labeled period. Who cares if ya gay straight bi black white yellow etc... How come people cant just be people? smdh
September 21, 2010 at 6:04pm · Like

116

**Darren Brax** Only. Because that's the world we live in, that is something that just can't be un-done, it's a good thing if you don't see color and don't care about what a person's sexual preference is but the majority of the people in the world think different, to me our differences is what makes us beautiful so in the end labels don't matter, it's all in God's hands in the end anyway, our focus really doesn't need to be on the labels because we know for a fact that won't change, but hopefully homosexuals will one day have equal rights
September 21, 2010 at 7:11pm · Like

**Natasha T. Miller** Its sad when you can't openly die for something you love. You have to fight for your country and possibly get killed with no honor. The best wars are won by honest soldiers and America is asking us to lie to them while fighting for the? It makes no sense. Where is the progress? Spare me the reward of a purple heart, where are the red ones, the ones that love and care about humanity back. There is no freedom in taking away rights, and there is no bravery in fearing freedom.
September 21, 2010 at 11:41pm · Like · 4 people

Write a comment...

**Natasha T. Miller**

A Judge has ordered the military to stop enforcing the "don't ask, don't tell policy" a day after national coming out day; keep making noise and being heard. Don't be forced to keep you to yourself.

October 12, 2010 at 5:23pm via iPhone · Like · Comment

👍 Katie Arnold, Adrienne Roach, Bridget Grubbs-Carter and 23 others like this.

 **Nkenge Jazz Browner** Amen...the silence is literally killing us
October 12, 2010 at 5:35pm · Like

 **Candace Johnson** LITERALLY. BUT,SOME PEOPLE WANT TO JUST KEEP ON COMPLAINING ABOUT THE GAYS. EVEN OUR 'FRIENDS'.
October 12, 2010 at 5:37pm · Like

Write a comment...

**Natasha T. Miller**
Heterosexual men: do you think you can turn a lesbian woman back hetero? If so why?
September 14, 2010 at 10:00am via iPhone · Like · comment

**Delmar Quivens** ha ha ha. Im sure thats not supposed to be funny but if she is a real lesbian than thats like turning lead into gold it cant be done. Its not a choice its who they are. As far as the lead gold thing I dont think lesbians are lead or gold... Im just saying. :0)
September 14, 2010 at 10:02am · Like · 5 people

**Sheryl Elys** whats a real lesbian?^
September 14, 2010 at 10:04am · Like

**Andrew Cloud** I think it depends on the woman. There are some lesbian women, who honestly have no desire for men in any way shape or form. But there are some who are curious. I don't believe that curiosity is enough to turn a lesbian woman straight. She will either return back to lesbianism or become bi-sexual.
September 14, 2010 at 10:10am · Like · 1 person

**Eli Gray** It's uhh...not really anyones choice. Am I missing something?
September 14, 2010 at 10:11am · Like

**Laurica Stone** The hetero man who thinks he can turn a lesbian str8 is on ego overload and has that domineering aspect on life. They prolly think their penis is the exception to the rule. Lol. Smh.
September 14, 2010 at 10:23am · Like · 1 person

119

**Natasha T. Miller** I often hear men say "I can turn her back" assuming that she was heterosexual first, so I question what methods can be used to do this?
September 14, 2010 at 10:25am · Like · 3 people

**Sherry Smith** How can you turn a lesbian back straight if she was never straight to begin with? Its like turning a chicken into a rooster, when it was never a rooster in the first place. This notion of all lesbians are really heterosexual women and they have just been "turned out" by a woman is crazy. When are people going to start accepting that some are born this way..?? I have a low tolerance for ignorance, men who pursue women knowing they have little chance but big hopes for turning them back straight get no respect from me.
September 14, 2010 at 10:53am · Like · 2 people

**K.Angela Feeman** ...what Delmar said! :)
September 14, 2010 at 10:58am · Like

**Krista Brax** I agree with Delmar! Wonderful topic! Although I'm not a heterosexual man, lol, I have had this conversation with Doug since I formerly liked chics. His opinion was similar to Darryl. I would like to say to all guys that may visit this status, that if those words ever come out of your mouth to a lesbian or female who thinks she likes girls because thats all she ever had (there is a difference and thats what i was), it is the most unattractive thing that one could say and I have never seen a guy "make" a woman do anything she doesn't want to do herself ;)
September 14, 2010 at 11:05am · Like

**Antwan Poll** I don't think a man can change a lesbian woman back to be heterosexual. Only her experience and curiosity can do that
September 14, 2010 at 11:14am · Like

120

**Bradley Forts** I dont think you can turn anyone into anything by..they are who they are...but i do believe you can get someone to love you for who you are or who they think you are...sex is sex..gay or straight...but love...fallin in love with someone is a different thing...i think that plays on both side of the fence. sexual orientation, race, religion, etc. That love shit is dangerous...it turns a lot of people into a lot of things. So no, a heterosexual man doesnt have the power or prowess to turn a lesbian woman straight...but if there is a since of genuine honesty, trust, and sincerity between the two...then love could form...be it plutonic or serious. Please dont bash me...just my opinion
September 14, 2010 at 11:27am · Like · 3 people

**Natasha T. Miller** @bradley that's a really good take on it. Most people limit there response/opinion to sex. Now when you throw love in there things change, especially if you truly believe that love has no shape, gender, race ect. Which is why people state that you can't help who you love. You're right for reasons like this, we further comprehend the dangers of love. It's scary to think that love has the power to change everything you are, think you are, or wanna be.
September 14, 2010 at 11:38am · Like · 2 people

**Bradley Forts** thats what i was trying to say....thats why you the shit....thats why i love you mama!
September 14, 2010 at 11:40am · Like

**Darren Brax** Some women who are living the lesbian life are still attracted to men,but they keep it on the low,I feel that women who have always been attracted to women can never go to being with a man,but women who turned gay for whatever the reason is can go back to being with men,it's not what the man is doing at allso you can't turn anyone straight or gay,that's a decision people make
September 16, 2010 at 12:11am · Like

Write a comment...

121

**Natasha T. Miller**
Spare me the reward of a purple heart, where are the red ones, the ones that love and care about humanity back: There is no freedom in taking away rights, there is no bravery in fearing freedom.

**Natasha T. Miller**
Excuse my confusion but I thought that president Obama wanted to do as much as he could to protect the rights of homosexuals. If this is true, why would his administration file an emergency request to keep the "don't as don't tell" policy in place after it's been removed?! Dear President Obama, You are a white house dressed as a white flag. You are not as peaceful as you speak sir.
October 20, 2010 at 3:45pm via iPhone · Like ·comment
22 others like this.

**Eran Ramens** I really think alot of things are beyond his control. The white hose is subsequently ran by the ideals of a higher power. There are forces that have always been in place that illiminated the right of people of color...its just a more advance approach where even then the president didnt control the choices that illegally violated the rights of many people in which the laws refuse to protect them. With all do respect it your choice to feel but try to understand that its not obama acting along.
October 20, 2010 at 3:56pm · Like · 1 person

**Natasha T. Miller** And that would be the expected argument. Everything is "out of his control" it seems as if the only things we want to hold him responsible for are the things that are pleasing to us. It's his administration and he knew the politics of presidency before he became president and with that being said, HE shouldn't have promised us things that he knew would never be reality. I don't, so much mind people not doing what they said as much as I mind them doing the complete opposite of what they said!
October 20, 2010 at 4:01pm · Like · 6 people

**Dara Wykes** u dnt unstand tasha the dnt ask dnt tell is helping gays because if they know they wont let ppl in!
October 20, 2010 at 4:16pm · Like

**Sheryl Elys** We wear the mask.

123

October 20, 2010 at 4:25pm · Like

**Eran Ramens** wow we have a lot to be greatful for. People are looseing everything they got due to the bush adminastration. Yet on top of all the challenges that obama face only so much can be worked out. Also you must consider whats tied into your request. Who else is supporting it with their agendas. There are a lot of tactic implied by sneaky underhanded politics and that use the emotions of a cause to stimulate their plot. If you dont like obama you just dont like him but dont believe that he controls the office of presidency...please its much more advanced than that.
October 20, 2010 at 5:00pm · Like · 1 person

**Asta Marcy** I think that homosexuals should be allowed to serve, but I wonder if the don't ask, don't tell idea keeps them safe from homophobic idiots who might set them up for all manor of evil. If you have everyday citizens walking around homophobic enough to beat someone and leave them for dead how much worse can it be when you lock them up in a "locker room full of jocks" type situation with trained killers? I don't know. I think it might actually be a good thing to keep folks out of their business.
October 20, 2010 at 6:29pm · Like · 2 people

**Eran Ramens** Ms Marcy your right but to those who are religious they know that god protects his own. Maybe...just maybe this is a form of protection that will shelter unnecessary issue that will disorganize the military. Do as dont tell is surely an apparent notion that will set gays up for farther heart break. If you can recall history with the situation of the tuskgee air men and the naval unite that would not except the black man sharing quarters but was honored that he we give his blood in a war that wouldnt give him the same freedom that they were fighting with
October 20, 2010 at 8:20pm · Like · 1 person

Write a comment...

124

## New message

To | Enter a friend's name or email address

Message | CHAPTER6
When the robot starts to speak or malfunction, we panic: We have forgotten that our athletes are people and some of our athletes have forgotten that their fans are people, with feelings, and struggles outside of sports. The moment you are paid to be a public figure is the moment that you are paid to influence, whether you accept it or not. We all know that with greatness comes responsibility and that responsibility should be present always, on the court, on the field, in the pool, on the track, holding a racket, holding a bat, losing or winning a game.

Send   Cancel

**Natasha T. Miller**
What are your thoughts on Kobe Bryant calling the referee a faggot?
What do you think the penalty should have been or do you think
there should have been one?
Yesterday at 4:00pm · Like ·comment
Tabitha, Anderson and  ControverSi  like this.

**Utoma Olae** I think that in the heat of any game, there are things that
are said to hurt people even if you don't mean it. That is part of every sport and
can be considered unsportsmanlike or simply competitive. I don't believe that he
should have charged a $100,000 fine though. Freedom to express one's anger
should not be punished with a fine.
Yesterday at 4:05pm · Like

**Natasha T. Miller** so playing sports gives you a pass to be openly
offensive when angry? Weren't we all taught to not say things that we mean?
who gives you the freedom to express anger?
Yesterday at 4:08pm · Like · 3 people

**Tony Bick** freedom to express one's anger isn't a pass for hate
speech.
Yesterday at 4:11pm · Like · 3 people

**Bree  Badazz** If thats the case there should be a fine for everything
you do.! The amendment is freedom of speech and thats what ppl use; it
would've been different if it was racists but a faggot..! Wow over board..!!!
Yesterday at 4:15pm · Like

**Natasha T. Miller** so you don't think that the word faggot is as

126

offensive as a racial slur to some folks? who determines the sting of the word? I assume its the people that care nothing about being called the word.
Yesterday at 4:17pm · Like · 7 people

**Utoma Olae** People say things out of anger all the time. Does it give you a pass? No. Does it mean that you should be penalized for being human? No. Just because he's an athlete doesn't mean that he should be punished for something that any one of us would say when we're angry and not mean in a derogatory way. The only reason this even got escalated this bad is because the ref is gay. If he wasn't, this wouldn't have even made news. Just another attempt to fool Americans into paying attention to something pointless in our own country while all hell breaks out everywhere else.
Yesterday at 4:18pm · Like · 1 person

**Utoma Olae** I feel that faggot and racial slurs are similar, although bearing a different past. But.....who has the right to fine someone for speaking out of anger? An emotion that does not allow people to think rationally?
Yesterday at 4:19pm · Like

**Nova Roswell** I don't think it was meant as in him talking about gay people, and I'm gay myself. I understand people are upset nut it wasn't necessary to do all that they are doing
Yesterday at 4:19pm · Like · 1 person

**Rockie Amenson** Expressing your anger is on thing...so it would have been ok if he was white and called a blk ref a n!663r? That's expressing your anger in some eyes and prejudice in others. He got what he deserved...$100,000 fine! I bet he'll think b4 he speak next time.
Yesterday at 4:21pm · Like · 4 people

**Rockie Amenson** Oan, He called a ref a fag...but he's the biggest cry baby in the NBA...smh
Yesterday at 4:23pm · Like

127

**Justine 'Jue M' Merdue** Playin sports does not give u the right 2 be openly offensive, and yes a lot of emotions r flowin whhen we play but u still have to be aware of the things u say esp professionally. He is a public figure & should have known that someone would hear what he said. He should have been fined bc those type of actions should never b tolerated. If he wasnt punished then that would just show younger ppl that it is ok to say hurtful things & when u become a professional u can get away wit it which is the wrong message to send whether u really meant to offend someone or not! Just bc he's Kobe doesnt make him exempt from punishment.
Yesterday at 4:24pm · Like · 1 person

**Utoma Olae** Yes, because everyone stops their emotions when they get fined $100k. How many times have people been punished publicly and still do the crime? This is NBA's way of saving face. It has nothing to do with what is right. And if you paid attention to the news you would have seen the apologies and the fake "make this right" stuff. And you stating that example is exactly my point. If you can make something of it, it's news, but if it was a gay baller who said fag, even if it is still offensive, it wouldn't have made a difference.
Yesterday at 4:25pm · Like

**Rockie Amenson** Freedom of speech does not mean the freedom to ofend ones sexual preference...
Yesterday at 4:28pm · Like

**Utoma Olae** So because you may be a local image to the kids in your neighborhood, that means that you can't be a normal human being, make mistakes, or speak your mind about how you feel towards something in public that may negatively impact how those kids look at you? How about we stop placing celebrities on pedestals people. He said some shit, he apologized...you want him to play the next game in a dress to show he doesn't hate homosexuals too?
Yesterday at 4:28pm · Like

**Nova Roswell** Then eveyone should get fined whenever a curse word

128

comes out. He not exempt from anything but a lot of things are offensive and they don't get in trouble for them consistently. So if we gonna fine people I'm just sting they need to be consistent everytime some "mouths" something. They pick and choose who they wanna put out ther and it happened to be his turn..... He has probably said it a million other times, the camera just happenedd to be in his mouth so they had to do something to appease the public
Yesterday at 4:29pm · Like

**Sheryl Elys** Some body please send me my registration for the prejudice olympics... How can you really compare HATE??? So what of the gay Black Lakers fan, he wasn't called the N word so, he shouldn't be upset ? ...hurt? Offended? He was dead wrong, we defend each other at all cost, sometimes to the detriment of what we really believe. If I was a GAY season ticket holder, I would have wanted to see him fined. Black people hate racism being compared to homophobia but always doing it themselves... SingMH! It was hate speech Kobe is a role model like it or not. If he dont like it tell him to stop hawking shoes.
Yesterday at 4:31pm · Like

**Briane Verux** Anything you say to intentionally put someone down is (ALWAYS) wrong but there were probably a hundred fans yelling the same thing at the teams and the referees, Have they been fined? I can understand if they suspended him because of his conduct but a monetary fine just seems like they wanted a reason to get money. What would hurt more is to actually take him out of the game for more than one night. To show him that he cant do things like that during the game. He has to conduct himself in a better manner because basketball isn't just a sport it's a business and I wouldn't do that on my job and neither should he.
Yesterday at 4:32pm · Like

**Sheryl Elys** They should donate the money to organizations and programs for gay Black men and boys...
Yesterday at 4:32pm · Like · 2 people

**Utoma Olae** IF YOU PEOPLE WANNA GET UPSET ABOUT HIM SAYING A HATE WORD, HOW COME NOBODY'S UPSET THAT THE SHOES THEY ARE ALL WEARING COME FROM THE BLOOD AND SWEAT OF CHILDREN OVERSEAS WHO

WORK ENDLESS DAYS FOR LESS THAN A DOLLAR?! You want to make a big deal out this little shit, why not focus on the bigger picture. Yeah, you'll fine him, he'll apologize and 3 years later, just like everything else with EVERY OTHER FUCKING CELEBRITY, it'll disappear until the next time you wikipedia his name.
Yesterday at 4:35pm · Like · 4 people

**Nova Roswell** N word, faggot, its all the same. I just feel EVERYONE should be fined then. And if it wa consistent, then there would be a fine in EVERY game. Sports is a business and like a said before had the camera not caught him it would have continued like a normal day, but because it did they had to do something before GLAAD or the human rights advocates said something. This was just their way of saving they own ass
Yesterday at 4:38pm · Like

**Utoma Olae** Everyone wants to act all high and mighty saying that he deserves it, blah blah blah. Let's put some biblical shit on the table right now. "He who is without sin cast the first stone." Which one of you can say that you're so perfect that you can say that his mistake is unacceptable? That he deserves to be punished because YOU never did it anything remotely similar? Or are you gonna tell me that you're different because there isn't 100 million people that know you exist? You want to fix the celebrities? Fix yourself, fix your community, and then take that solution globally. But you won't. So keep on bitching about a change that you aren't willing to invoke yourself.
Yesterday at 4:38pm · Like

**Nova Roswell** Utoma I definitely agree that this thing with kobe was blown out of proportion.
Yesterday at 4:42pm · Like · 1 person

**Sheryl Elys** eff that bible shit... we do care about sweatshop labor... you don't know us all. 100,000 dollars to Kobe is like ten to me lets keep it real. We get fined for illegal things we do all the time. effing F@gg*t is a big deal on national t.v. for the swear word alone. Then add the misplaced affinity for words that equate hate speech and its a valid enforceable reason to fine the man. Fining him was a message unfortunately we always the ones being made an example but he said it. He is a professional Basketball player. If I called the quality assurance place at my job and said what he said, I'd be fired.

130

**Utoma Olae** Everything with any celebrity is blown out of proportion. They get treated like gods so we watch their every move and capitalize on what we can. I swear to God, if Vanilla Ice cream was considered a stamina booster, and michael jordan was seen walking out of baskin robbins with his kids, we'd be talking about whether or not his performance on the court wasn't enhanced. Meanwhile, when was the last update on Japan, how's India doing? What's the latest news on the Middle East? How much can we know about the outside world without having to go to a foreign country's news website? Oh, but since that shit wasn't on NBC it doesn't matter. Kobe saying a hate word out of animosity because he doesn't know how to shut his mouth when he's pissed off about something he's passionate about: that's what really makes news.
Yesterday at 4:46pm · Like · 1 person

**Utoma Olae** Sheryl, you may care about it, but that's not the topic of discussion. Nobody got upset when the newest Jordans came out and they were made by Nike. When I say nobody, I mean the mass, the populous, not one person. The simple fact that we can have a 30min discussion about whether or not Kobe was in the wrong but no one brings up the millions of other things that wrong with our country in regards to what we support...is THE REAL PROBLEM.

Yeah, Kobe is wealthy as hell. But if someone tried to take $10 from me, and I work my ass off to make that measly $10, I'd be pissed. And if you said that at work, you would be fired....but only if there was enough of a big deal brought up to do something about it. Hence, Don Imus.
Yesterday at 4:51pm · Like

**Nova Roswell** Yes!
Yesterday at 4:52pm · Like

**Sheryl Elys** You brought it up! I hate when people comment on celebrity based statuses and then be like we shouldn't even be talking about this there are larger ills at hand. True there are. We can't deal with all of the issues that are important to us? This is important to me. Me and my five year old son was watching that game, I don't want him to think its cool to say that phrase. I know many will say its how you raise your kids but deny they are influenced by

131

outside factors is preposterous. I didn't need to hear him say it. You are bringing up issues important to you and that is valid but this not your status
Yesterday at 4:56pm · Like · 1 person

**Utoma Olae** I did bring it up. Because that's more impactful on our society than one popular guy saying a hate word that you couldn't really hear because of all the other people yelling and booing at the same time. You could read his lips, but you couldn't hear it.
Yesterday at 4:59pm · Like

**Rockie Amenson** I had to get off my smart/dum phone and access my laptop. Lol. First off Kobe Bryant isn't just one of us "normal" people...he made the choice to be in the spot light so therefore he has to watch what he says. Not only that he has to remember who he is and what he represents!(Just like Dog the Bounty Hunter) So, the refree was really "gay" the proper term...so, he did mean to say it, if it was out of angry or not that was his personal opinion to say it so it was the NBA personal opinion to fine him!
Yesterday at 5:00pm · Like

**Utoma Olae** And I didn't say we shouldn't be talking about this, I said it isn't worth talking about. Does this have an impact on our younger society? Yeah, but what Kobe says doesn't do shit compared to every other outlet of media in the world. That's like saying "good job on fining Kobe!!! Hahaha.....Gucci said nigger again." You can't get mad at one person, or one source of media, and let everyone else get a pass. I'm agreeing 100% with Nina: the only reason why people are making a big deal out of this is because 1) He got caught and 2) He's fucking Kobe.
Yesterday at 5:02pm · Like

**Utoma Olae** Rockie, people say faggot to straight people all the time. And that still has the same effect to a hetero as it does a homo. If the ref was straight, this still would have been blown up. Wanna know why? Because in none of the reports, news articles or anything else with the exception to yahoo answers, did I see any mention of the referee being gay. It's not who he said it to, it's what he said. Don Imus could've called a bunch of white girls nappy headed hoes and that shit still would have went down.
Yesterday at 5:05pm · Like · 1 person

**Justine 'Jue M' Merdue** I simply stated my opinion and who's really upset? True enough it may not have been that serious to some ppl but 4 the ppl it could have offended they handled the situation. I believe celebrities are human just as we r but we cant ignore the fact that ppl see them in a diff light. Yes we all sin but who want as far 2 actually put the bible in the situation?! It's not fair but unfortunately he was caught, not everything can be caught or be handled. Imagine the hassle of tryin to fine every like action but when it's highly offensive to a mass of ppl it may need to be handled differently. Ok he apologized but that wasnt enough to just let it go under the radar has fine didnt burn a hole in his pocket!
Yesterday at 5:06pm · Like · 1 person

**Rockie Amenson** If it's not worth talking about, why are you still commenting? Just because we all have different opinions on what happened DOES NOT mean anyone is gettting upset or mad. No, no one is without sin...we were born in sin and will die in sin! So, no one can't cast any stones but we do have a right to our opinions. Yes the media has blown it out of proportion like they do everything else! Prejudice is prejudice and he chose to let that derogatory statement fly loosely so he should not have a problem letting that $$$ fly so loosely! LMAO
Yesterday at 5:18pm · Like · 1 person

**Utoma Olae** So we should strip him of his wealth to prove that what did was wrong? And exactly how does that seem fair? Because he's rich and famous he should be fined? Wow, that sounds similar to the VERY THING WE'RE ARGUING ABOUT RIGHT NOW!!! And I went as far as to put the bible into this. Because the only accurate way to judge someone is from a source of purity, and the bible, Qu'ran and Miqra are the three most prominent in that category. So if everyone here feels like they can point their fingers and pass judgment, then why can't I use a book that this country built its foundation of justice on as a devil's advocate to the very hypocrites that feel they have a right to act like they know better?
Yesterday at 5:18pm · Like

**Utoma Olae** You're right about one thing: this isn't worth discussing anymore. This is a blinding argument, and I still have enough sight to see my

133

way out of it.
Yesterday at 5:21pm · Like · 1 person

**Shea** A real fine that he would've noticed
Yesterday at 5:24pm · Like

**Rockie Amenson** And a $100,000 aint puttin a dent in his pockets!
Lol
Yesterday at 5:30pm · Like

**Shea** If the ref would've brought up his drama he would've been replaced for being unprofessional & they would've made up a bunch of bull to keep Kobe happy..me personally think he let himself out with that one Okaay..lol 4real!
Yesterday at 5:32pm · Like · 1 person

**Delmar Quivens** If I said something racist on the street I might get my butt kicked. Say it at work might get fired. Say it while on TV might get sued. The bigger your audience the more impact and problem it is. There are checks and balances with everything and you cant just run off at the mouth because your angry for any reason. What if he had said Im glad Katrina and Japan situations happened to weed out the week and said it to a bi racial ( black and asian person ) Would it be wrong? What if when Bush was president ( and angry ) he said I hate Ni%%ers... Would he be impeached? If someone doesn't tell people that its wrong then no one will stop. Just apologizing doesn't' seem to stop him so maybe a fine is in order. There is an expectation that if your on live TV that you are respectful and if your not then you will pay the price... He did.
Yesterday at 5:44pm · Like · 1 person

**Rockie Amenson** Well said! ^
Yesterday at 5:50pm · Like

134

**Ini Black** Was he wrong? Absolutely. Should he have been fined? Not in my opinion. We have ALL said things we shouldn't have, anyone who says otherwise is lying. There have been MANYYYYY celebrities who have yelled all type of offensive, out of pocket, sexist, racist remarks...and I didn't hear about any of them being fined. Regardless, I don't agree that just because someone is a "professional" and has a lot of money means they should have harsher consequences for their actions than anyone else. People can say whatever they want, we don't have to like it...I most def don't...but thats life. When people show you who they are, believe them.
Yesterday at 5:53pm · Like · 1 person

**Natasha T. Miller** so should we have swept it under the rug and kept it moving? when a person tells me what shouldn't have happened I am always compelled to ask what should have happened? since we cant catch and find everybody, should we let everyone that we can make an example out of go? do we say kobe you were wrong but we all are wrong at some point in our lives so just say you're sorry and get back to the game? Do I think the fine was necessary? yes Do I think the fine should've went back to the NBA? No. I think the money should've been donated to help the cause that he cared nothing about hurting.
Yesterday at 5:59pm · Like · 2 people

**Utoma Olae** I can't even look away from that one. Who said that? Who said that you must be respectful on live TV? Where is that written in their contracts, the social media unwritten laws of public tv? It isn't. It's an opinion, and a bullshit one at that. Okay, yeah, Kobe deserves a fine. Where's the fine for the rappers, the hip hop artists, the Comedians who drop racial slurs for laughs? Oh that shit's acceptable because that's in their job description to be secular and insulting, but because Kobe doesn't need to SAY anything in his job that's where the problem lies? What makes Kobe any different from every other person who came before him and did/said the same thing publicly? If Kobe was a bench warmer and the camera saw that, you think it would have been the same response? Are you kidding me?! So if it's a racial slur or hate word it's acceptable, so he can curse at the ref as much as he wants? That must be the case. Because only when sensitive topics are discussed does that pose an issue. You're comparing a basketball player to the president of the United States. Since when did the two hold the same weight, the same responsibilities? As a president, you represent the WHOLE COUNTRY. Kobe represents Kobe. That's like saying it's our right to get upset at Tiger Woods for sleeping around. If he wants to fuck other women, who are we to say shame on you?! That's none of

135

our business lol. The same way it's none of our business what a celebrity says on public tv. That's his problem not ours. When a person represents us says something like that, then it's a different story.

If you honestly believe you can control yourself when you're angry, then you've never been angry. Plain and simple. You may have been really upset, but anger, true anger, is not something that can be controlled at all times. And let's get one thing clear: just because they are watched by the media, does not mean that they should behave any differently. If you were being watched 24 hours a day does that mean you're not gonna take shower or take a piss because that type of image is inappropriate when shown to children? Yeah saying something out of anger doesn't justify it. i'll agree. But judging someone from what they said when they were angry isn't a valid phrase to stand by either. He paid the price, someone made a stand. And in another year or so, it'll happen again, and again, and again.

You say that if someone doesn't tell people it's wrong then they won't stop. So what's the point in only telling one out of hundreds of people who do it?
Yesterday at 6:06pm · Like

**Ini Black**  Nah, I dont think it should have been swept under the rug. But I am always confused when our first response is to punish people in the form of money. That makes absolutely no sense to me. Who is that benefiting and what lesson is being taught? Also,that lil bit of money means nothing to Kobe. I dont think it will cause him to 'think twice' about using the word again. If anything, send him to some type of program where he's forced to interact with people who are different..not even in hopes that he come to agree with homosexuality (because its not for him to "agree" with anyway) but perhaps he would at least learn something as simple as respect-regardless of your personal feelings toward someoone/something, regardless if you are 'angry'...respect. Or maybe not..but at least him being forced to do something such as that would put emphasis on the root of what the problem is.
Yesterday at 6:06pm · Like · 1 person

**Ini Black**  And honestly..the penalty that i described above would probably only happen in an ideal world that we dont live in.
Yesterday at 6:07pm · Like · 1 person

**Natasha T. Miller**  I agree, taking money doesn't seem like it would hurt or make a person in his tax bracket change but then again, I don't know

136

how much kpbe loves his money so I can't be correct about what it will or will not do to or for him. @Ini I agree with your solution. I think something involving time spent and not money would've been better but David stearn makes the rules in the NBA and I'm a tad bit satisfied with him taking some kind of action. I think he should've gotten suspended, show him what it feels like to have something you love taken away from you but that wasn't the outcome and unfortunately we had no say so in it. We disagree with the consequence but that doesn't make it the wrong one.
Yesterday at 6:14pm · Like · 2 people

**Delmar Quivens** when you go to a venue where you expect cursing people will curse ( Comedy shows, Jerry springer ) When you go to hockey you expect people to fight ( I personally think its unacceptable ) When you go to a basketball game you expect people to play ball... Everyone gets upset but there is a time and a place for everything. If Im angry as hell at a judge for giving me a ticket I dont think I deserve and I call him a name Im going to jail...
Yesterday at 6:15pm · Like

**Natasha T. Miller** I feel like Kobe Bryant could've articulated his anger much better. The word Faggot has nothing to do with being handed a technical foul.
Yesterday at 6:17pm · Like

**Delmar Quivens** With that same way of thinking Kobe is at work. Thats his job and at his job there isnt supposed to be that type of behavior. I think if he was on the street and said it then theres not much they can do but say man thats messed up. Same with Tiger... I dont know his home situation and its not my business I dont think its right that they put it out there. But if he is on whole 9 and he yells out thats why I f~d that *@^# then theres a problem.
Yesterday at 6:18pm · Like

**Utoma Olae** actually, if you call a judge a name, you get warned first. If you disregard that warning, then you are thrown in jail for being disorderly. You're given a warning even when in front of a judge. And if you go to any event, if all you look at is the event itself then that's all you'll see. But if you wandered behind the scenes or walked into the restroom and saw them taking a shot of jack daniels or shooting up in their locker room does that mean they

137

should be fired because they were doing it away from where they perform?
Yesterday at 6:19pm · Like

**Raven Wesley** He should have been punished for saying the word. I think its interesting that everyone in the post when referencing the N-Word does not even dare type it –not even me– but everyone so freely types the slur Kobe used. That's part of the problem–I say the media should wrap this word in stigma–a big deal should be made out of this–it shouldn't be so comfortable to say or to write–it is hate speech. One of the responsibilities of fame (and getting grossly over paid more than teachers and public servants) is that you're moves are watched. He can afford this fine no sweat. It should be donated to a shelter that helps young homosexuals that have been kicked out of their homes. Kobe should clock some hours in a place like that too.
Yesterday at 6:22pm · Unlike · 1 person

**Utoma Olae** Now we can agree upon something. KOBE IS AT WORK. His job is to play ball, not be a beacon of light, not be an image for kids to look up to, and not be a media scape goat. When Kobe is at work, he does his job. He plays ball. The same way that when you're at work, you're not paying attention to the security camera that might be watching you pick your nose and shake your bosses hand. Every keeps saying the same thing: that you should be respectful on tv. Exactly how many of you think that every time a celebrity goes to work he's focused on his job and prying eyes? As if they don't have enough pressure you think that they need to add the thought that they're being watched 24/7 to that list as well? No, they don't. Not everyone asks for fame. But that's what pays the rent. Without it, tickets don't sell, seats don't get filled, and contracts don't get renewed. It is not their responsibility to watch what they say. It's their agents. Because that, is THEIR job. If this wasn't live, and Kobe's agent bought that tape off the guy who filmed it, nobody would be talking about what celebrities should(n't) say on live tv.
Yesterday at 6:26pm · Like

**Delmar Quivens** I used to be HR for a big company and if you did something like this while at work or on company grounds you would be fired or suspended. Im not a sports expert but I would say he would lose more money being suspended even one game.
Yesterday at 6:27pm · Like

**Utoma Olae** And if Tiger Woods said "that's why I screwed that chick" on live tv, would that be just as unacceptable if he swore? Once again, it's none of our business. We watch him play the game, no one looks at celebs to see when next they're gonna fuck up.
Yesterday at 6:27pm · Like

**Raven Wesley** No–I am sorry Kobe's job is not just to play ball–it became more than that when he started accepting endorsements. He has made himself a brand, a face for things, he has more responsibility than just playing ball–which he gets paid NICELY for.
Yesterday at 6:29pm · Like

**Natasha T. Miller** There is a code of conduct enforced when playing in the NBA and it clearly states that players will respect and appreciate every fan. he clearly went against the code.
Yesterday at 6:29pm · Like · 1 person

**Utoma Olae** He would. And if this was truly that big of a deal, then that's what would have been done. But it isn't. Which is why he was only fine $100k. You want to make a change, you make an impact. There was no impact, so there will be no change. All these people saying he deserved that fine, it's kinda sad that you think that's all it takes to make a stand. The fine is meaningless. Just to save face. I wouldn't be surprised if the fine was only on paper and it never happened.
Yesterday at 6:30pm · Like

**Delmar Quivens** And I agree that thats the way it goes down normally. The agent makes it go away but if the regulators of the whole thing say he shouldnt do it shouldnt he not do it? I mean if your boss says hey dont yell at customers but you have a friend in security that can change the tape out if you do should you keep doing it because you can?
Yesterday at 6:31pm · Like

**Natasha T. Miller** but who are we to call the fine meaningless? we do not know how kobe felt about having HIS money taken away from him. maybe that 100k fine felt like jail for him, who are we to call it
Yesterday at 6:31pm · Like

**Utoma Olae** He became a brand and face for PRODUCT BASED ON THE FACT THAT HE PLAYS BALL. That has nothing to do with his original job, it just encourages him to continue it. His job is still just playing ball.
@T Miller, the same way we can't call his fine meaningless, is the same way we have no right to judge his actions either. For any form of judgment would require power or deity, and I think it's safe to assume that we have none of that.
@Darryl, if your boss says don't do it, and you don't do it, and then you slip up, and your boss doesn't care, then you slip up and get caught by your boss and get punished for it, is it your fault for getting caught or your bosses fault for not nipping it in the bud the first time?
Yesterday at 6:35pm · Like

**Delmar Quivens** Mine for doing it. I am responsible for me. If I know its wrong its wrong no matter whos watching and if I get caught I pay the price what ever it may have been predeternmined to be.
Yesterday at 6:39pm · Like

**Utoma Olae** And does that mean that if others who have done the same thing find out you've done it, have the right to judge you as well?
Yesterday at 6:42pm · Like

**Natasha T. Miller** He went against his contract so we can judge his actions. You think his endorsements only have to do with his talent? why do you think tiger lost endorsements after his blow out? why do you think Kobe lost his show deal after he was accused of rape? its not just about the talent sir. you represent the people, the people who pay you to represent you and do what you love.
Yesterday at 6:44pm · Like

140

**Delmar Quivens** Its not their business but if I do it to where all my co workers and customers can see then yes they have the right to talk about me. But at work on company hours they are held to the same standards. So if Im mad and get on the loud speaker and chew someone out... I get fired. If my co workers heard I would expect them to talk about me and the situation ( I was dumb for being wrong on the loud speaker ) But while we are at work if they talk about me worse then what the company allows then they get fired too. Accountability.
Yesterday at 6:47pm · Like

**Utoma Olae** Tiger lost some of his endorsements because the companies felt that having him under their label would be negative towards business. Another company, EA, did not believe this at all, and quoted on record "that we will not be dropping Tiger Woods from our company.....and hope that he can get through this ordeal." EA's stock has risen since then. The reason why companies drop celebs is to save face, not because they disagree with what they've done. It's a business move, based on inconclusive results. If they knew that they would keep their stock up after all the jazz that happens with any celeb, they would. If he somehow lost his ability to play, then they would drop him for sure because he can't live up to the original agreement.

And so because he broke his contract we can judge. But we haven't broken any contracts? We haven't pledged allegiance to our flag, and then said "America's fucking up" on a different day? We haven't sword to a religion and then either broken the pillars on which it stands, or denied it in its entirety? So we can fuck up and people can look at us and say "that's your choice" but when he does it we scream to the heavens? And the majority of those people....pay him to play. I could give a rat's ass what he says next week about Nigerians, but if he can score 30 points in a game, that's what I paid for. The problem is us. We're so nosy to the point that all of our actions are justified within ourselves that we can say our two cents about every one else. But it wouldn't be the same if you, T Miller, hold an unwritten contract, as a poet, to know what's going on with the world, and then you drop a piece saying I just want to be me, I don't give a damn about America or what's passed the Red Sea. How many people would judge you for that? Or would they just write it off as a intellectual way to say you're stressed out?

And Darryl, it's not their business. If it became gossip, it's not their business. If they overheard you doing it, it's not their business. Business is a contract between two or more parties with a direct effect to each member of that contract. If all they get out of it is something to talk about, then how is it any of their business? That's just being nosy.
Yesterday at 6:58pm · Like

141

**Joseph Palms** they use all type of language on the court, they caught a competitor in the heat of battle...believe they've said worst the fine was enough
Yesterday at 8:57pm · Like

**Tisha McKinley** wow... you can really tell how far removed some people still are from the discrimination of gays in america. the word faggot is just as bad as the word nigger. period
Yesterday at 10:26pm · Like

**Natasha T. Miller** @utoma, Im just reading your comment about "you people" getting upset about the word and not about where and how nikes are made. first, who are you people? the people on the opposing side? secondly, why is everything in comparison to something else, we are not talking about nikes, we are talking about the word faggot. I'm sure there are plenty of people right now on statuses, in front of sweat shops, tweeting, emailing, complaining and protesting the make of nikes but not here because that is not what we are talking about. The way nikes are made and the way we feel about how nikes are made is not going to change the way we feel about him using the word faggot. are you saying that one cause is bigger than the other? are you saying because we are not discussing that, we shouldn't be discussing his usage of the word? Please enlighten me, because now days it seems that in order for your anger about one thing to be validated, you have to be uncomfortable with something else, something more important to someone else. Maybe, just maybe, no one on this status cares about how nikes are made, or maybe everyone does but we just weren't discussing it because its not relevant to what we are discussing.
Yesterday at 11:04pm · Like · 2 people

**Utoma Olae** You people would be people on the imposing side.
12 hours ago · Like

**Natasha T. Miller** When I perform at open mics, I do not sign contracts but I am still respectful and mindful of my audience when performing.

142

When I perform at universities that require me to sign contracts, I follow the guidelines. If I choose to sign a contract to perform under certain guidelines and I violate my contract and get fined, I will not complain because I knew what terms I was agreeing to.
10 hours ago · Like

**Natasha T. Miller** Some folks did keep tiger woods under their wings but some didn't and we cant be mad at the ones who chose to give him the boot because of his actions. being nosey? uh, you are aware that he was playing basketball on national TV right? In front of kids, Adults, Americans, homosexuals, christians, nosey folks, folks who just wanted to see the game and a world full of all types of people?! Yea, I don't think that was being nosey, I think that was watching the game; The game that he chose to play in from of millions of people. Millions of people that he agreed to respect when signing his contract. If I openly offend one person or a group of people and Im called out for it, I will not complain.
10 hours ago · Like

Write a comment...

143

**jajapink** So because he surgical change himself into a woman... he can play golf in the women's PGA?? #BullCrap
15 Oct Favorite Reply

**Mic_Phelps** Microphone Phelps @jajapink RIGHT lol YOU are NOT a WOMAN! Just a fuck nigga playn golf with women lol 15 Oct **Favorite Retweet Reply**

**tmillerpoetry** natasha miller @jajapink @YoungPhenom so if she legally got a sex change that now identifies her as a woman, y wouldn't she be treated as such?
15 Oct Favorite Reply Delete

**Mic_Phelps** Microphone Phelps @tmillerpoetry @jajapink its not a SEX CHANGE ur still a male you just don't have a penis. SHE should play in the male league still
15 Oct **Favorite Retweet Reply**

**tmillerpoetry** natasha miller @jajapink @YoungPhenom I just don't think she received a sex change to still be treated as the sex she was before
15 Oct Favorite Reply Delete

**jajapink** @YoungPhenom: @tmillerpoetry O WOW I'm _____ lol but yea the problem is the unfair advantage
15 Oct Favorite Reply

**Mic_Phelps** Microphone Phelps @tmillerpoetry @jajapink thats like if we really FELT INSIDE that we were teenagers and went and slammed for the youth team
15 Oct **Favorite Retweet Reply**

**Mic_Phelps** Microphone Phelps @tmillerpoetry @jajapink yeah i may be dressed like a kid, i may do all the things a kid does, but I"M NOT A KID.
15 Oct Favorite Retweet Reply

**tmillerpoetry** natasha miller @jajapink @YoungPhenom however I do believe that she should meet the leagues requirements such as weight, body mass ect
15 Oct Favorite Reply Delete

**Mic_Phelps** Microphone Phelps @@tmillerpoetry @jajapink its not about being respected as one. U can go to a woman's bathroom I'll CALL you female. But
15 Oct Favorite Retweet Reply

**Mic_Phelps** Microphone Phelps @tmillerpoetry @jajapink thats CHEATING! If Lebron James got his penis removed, should they let him in the WNBA?
15 Oct Favorite Undo Retweet Reply

**tmillerpoetry** natasha miller @jajapink @YoungPhenom but to say that she has the right to be physically turned into a woman but not respected as such is kinda rude.
15 Oct Favorite Reply Delete

**tmillerpoetry** natasha miller RT @YoungPhenom: @tmillerpoetry @jajapink thats like if we really FELT INSIDE that we were teenagers and went and slammed for the youth team
15 Oct Favorite Reply Delete

**tmillerpoetry** natasha miller @YoungPhenom that statement about teenagers

146

is really ignorant and I won't address it outside of this
15 Oct Favorite Reply Delete

**Mic_Phelps** Microphone Phelps @tmillerpoetry how is that IGNORANT? lol
It the same basic concept.
15 Oct Favorite Retweet Reply

**jajapink** @YoungPhenom: @tmillerpoetry as much as I would love to believe
that I can physically do everything a man can is just not true
15 Oct Favorite Reply

@YoungPhenom: @tmillerpoetry Men are stronger in most cases and have more weight
and muscle mass.
15 Oct Favorite Reply

**Mic_Phelps** Microphone Phelps @tmillerpoetry Why wouldn't he just play in
the NBA though? He's still a man, you can CALL him a woman. But he's still a MAN.
15 Oct Favorite Retweet Reply

**tmillerpoetry** natasha miller @YoungPhenom oh sir, how you so often
confuse rights with emotions and premature logic.
15 Oct Favorite Reply Delete

**Mic_Phelps** Microphone Phelps @tmillerpoetry @jajapink thats CHEATING!
If Lebron James got his penis removed, should they let him in the WNBA?

**tmillerpoetry** natasha miller @YoungPhenom if lebron is legally a woman and
meets the wnba requirements.
15 Oct Favorite Reply Delete

147

**Mic_Phelps** Microphone Phelps **@tmillerpoetry** if this is the case then a PENIS is what makes a man a man? Or a vagina makes a woman a woman.
15 Oct Favorite Retweet Reply

**jajapink** @YoungPhenom @tmillerpoetry When I have trouble opening the pickle jar I ask my dad to help not my mom
15 Oct Favorite Reply

**jajapink** @YoungPhenom: @tmillerpoetry I am all about respecting people but genetically he's a man u cant change that even if u clip the boobs &penis
15 Oct Favorite Reply

**jajapink** @YoungPhenom He will never fully be a woman. It's not possible

15 Oct Favorite Reply

**Mic_Phelps** Microphone Phelps **@jajapink** i feel like its almost like steroids real talk. Because you had to do something to physically set you apart to join this league

15 Oct Favorite Retweet Reply

**tmillerpoetry** natasha miller RT @jajapink: what if physically she has no advantages
15 Oct Favorite Reply Delete

**Mic_Phelps** Microphone Phelps **@jajapink** thats my thing because i feel like YOU"RE STILL A DUDE! I'll respect u and call u a woman, but I won't disrespect

15 Oct Favorite Retweet Reply

148

**Mic_Phelps** Microphone Phelps @jajapink these women by sayin, yeah even though im not a woman, I'm a woman. U can call him a woman. But he needs pills to be that fully
15 Oct **Favorite Retweet Reply**

**tmillerpoetry** natasha miller This is sad RT @jajapink: @tmillerpoetry as much as I would love to believe that I can physically do everything a man can is just not true
15 Oct Favorite Reply Delete

**tmillerpoetry** natasha miller @MoMochaLatte @YoungPhenom and that's why this transformation includes hormonal changes/pills that inserts more estrogen into the body
15 Oct Favorite Reply Delete

**Mic_Phelps** Microphone Phelps @jajapink its a complete change of a human being, which I have NOTHING against, its just tryin to play WOMAN'S golf with a man anatomy
15 Oct **Favorite Retweet Reply**

**tmillerpoetry** natasha miller
I can open a jar b4 some men RT @jajapink: @tmillerpoetry When I have trouble opening the pickle jar I ask my dad to help not my mom

15 Oct Favorite Reply Delete

**jajapink** @tmillerpoetry I can too after beating the lead, shaking it, and jumping on it. You eventually learn the science but as far as physically
15 Oct Favorite Reply

**jajapink** @tmillerpoetry My dad is naturally stronger
15 Oct Favorite Reply

**jajapink** @tmillerpoetry Woman can train and become strong as bulls but just speaking in general men are built stronger... And I know that there are

15 Oct Favorite Reply

**jajapink** @tmillerpoetry weak men and some can over power them but it's not the usual circumstance
15 Oct Favorite Reply

**Mic_Phelps** @tmillerpoetry @MoMochaLatte Well if she wants to play in a woman's golf league she can. But just know she is still a man
15 Oct Favorite Retweet Reply

**tmillerpoetry** @YoungPhenom so you'll call her a man for playing in the league but you will respect her and call her a woman outside of that
15 Oct Favorite Reply Delete

**Mic_Phelps** Microphone Phelps @tmillerpoetry yes because I'm not trying to tell her what she can't call her self. But in my eyes you're a MAN, but because what
15 Oct Favorite Retweet Reply

**jajapink** @jajapink: @tmillerpoetry @YoungPhenom When it comes to sports If they allow men to being in the women's arena. It should just be open game
15 Oct Favorite Reply

150

**Mic_Phelps** Microphone Phelps @tmillerpoetry @jajapink i bet i can open every can in yo house. Quicker than you

15 Oct **Favorite Retweet Reply**

**Mic_Phelps** Microphone Phelps @tmillerpoetry i mean a jar
15 Oct **Favorite Retweet Reply**

**tmillerpoetry** natasha miller And this may be so but some people mothers are stronger than their fathersAnd RT @jajapink: @tmillerpoetry My dad is naturally stronger
15 Oct Favorite Reply Delete

**Mic_Phelps** Microphone Phelps @tmillerpoetry I want to respect her I'll call her woman. Like I know ur name is Natasha, but if u wanted to be calld T I'd call you T
15 Oct **Favorite Undo Retweet Reply**

**tmillerpoetry** natasha miller @YoungPhenom I'm sure she didn't get a sex change to be CALLED a woman but to be treated as one
15 Oct Favorite Reply Delete

**tmillerpoetry** natasha miller @YoungPhenom I'm sure she didn't get a sex change to be CALLED a woman but to be treated as one
15 Oct Favorite Reply Delete

@YoungPhenom I would hope that if I made the decision to undergo surgery and

become a man, you Would do more than just CALL me that
15 Oct Favorite Reply Delete

**tmillerpoetry** natasha miller @YoungPhenom I would hope that you would respect my emotional transformation as well as my physical

**tmillerpoetry** natasha miller @YoungPhenom I'm saying: you do not have to agree with rights. You can think whatever for however long but u can't give me Half way rights
15 Oct Favorite Reply Delete

**Mic_Phelps** Microphone Phelps @tmillerpoetry its not about if I think she's a man or not. Its about what she chooses to be called. But I can think wat I'd like about her
15 Oct Favorite Retweet Reply

**tmillerpoetry** natasha miller @YoungPhenom I'm saying: you do not have to agree with rights. You can think whatever for however long but u can't give me Half my rights
15 Oct Favorite Reply Delete

**Mic_Phelps** Microphone Phelps @jajapink @tmillerpoetry I agree wit that
15 Oct Favorite Retweet Reply

**Mic_Phelps** Microphone Phelps @tmillerpoetry its not a half way right, I believe that u can get the procedure and all that, but ur still a GUY. So
15 Oct Favorite Retweet Reply

**Mic_Phelps** Microphone Phelps @tmillerpoetry and you can be treated like one. But no matter what there are always factors that play into everything.
15 Oct Favorite Retweet Reply

**Mic_Phelps** Microphone Phelps @tmillerpoetry Its not like sum1 is sayn u can't go to this bathroom, or I'm not callin u a woman. BUT its nothn wrong wit saying. 15 Oct **Favorite Retweet Reply**

**tmillerpoetry** natasha miller @YoungPhenom you'll let me use the womens bathroom but being treated like a woman in every area of my life is out of the question

15 Oct Favorite Reply Delete

**tmillerpoetry** natasha miller @YoungPhenom because you just don't BELIEVE that she should be Able to do everything that "real" women can do 15 Oct Favorite Reply Delete

**Mic_Phelps** Microphone Phelps @tmillerpoetry I would, but if u told me u wanted to play in the WNBA after u had ur transformation I'd be like I don't agree wit that T
15 Oct **Favorite Retweet Reply**

**tmillerpoetry** natasha miller @YoungPhenom If she is physically equal to the women in the league, and emotionally equal why wouldn't she be able to play? 15 Oct Favorite Reply Delete

**Mic_Phelps** Microphone Phelps @tmillerpoetry and on that same token I would hope that u would respect my choice to respect u but just not that one choice 15 Oct **Favorite Retweet Reply**

**tmillerpoetry** natasha miller @YoungPhenom because you just don't BELIEVE she should no matter what rights she is promised. Respect your beliefs but strongly Disagree.

**Mic_Phelps** Microphone Phelps @tmillerpoetry but in the long run it don't effect me, Im just saying that in my opinion you'll never BE a woman, u can act and look like
15 Oct **Favorite Retweet Reply**

**Mic_Phelps** Microphone Phelps @tmillerpoetry and feel like a woman but when you came out of a WOMAN you had a penis and you were a male.
15 Oct **Favorite Retweet Reply**

**Mic_Phelps** Microphone Phelps @tmillerpoetry but there is not WOMAN right or MALE right its just RIGHTS and you have the RIGHT to call urself watever. But SCIENCE will
15 Oct **Favorite Retweet Reply**

**Mic_Phelps** Microphone Phelps @tmillerpoetry tell you that no matter what you do to your body, you are still a MAN
15 Oct **Favorite Retweet Reply**

**tmillerpoetry** natasha miller @YoungPhenom it's so much easier to halfway support a movement as oppose to supporting it 100%.
15 Oct Favorite Reply Delete

**tmillerpoetry** natasha miller @YoungPhenom it's so much easier to talk about what it is, what it isn't and what it should be when IT doesn't directly affect your life.
15 Oct Favorite Reply Delete

**Mic_Phelps** Microphone Phelps @tmillerpoetry so let me ask you a question. After someone has a transformation would you say they are no longer in any from the other sex

15 Oct **Favorite Retweet Reply**

**tmillerpoetry** natasha miller @YoungPhenom yes I will. If a man emotionally feels like a woman and has a surgical procedure to match that emotion to me she is a woman

15 Oct Favorite Reply Delete

**tmillerpoetry** natasha miller @YoungPhenom  and vise versa. I will always respect a persons decision fully or not at all

15 Oct Favorite Reply Delete

**Mic_Phelps** Microphone Phelps @tmillerpoetry not really because now you have to try to stick to your beliefs WHILE RESPECTING someone else's rights. Not easy at all

15 Oct **Favorite Retweet Reply**

**tmillerpoetry** natasha miller @YoungPhenom that's why the extent of other people rights are usually based on the extent of other people beliefs

15 Oct Favorite Reply Delete

**Mic_Phelps** Microphone Phelps @tmillerpoetry he is no longer a man in any way shape of form?

15 Oct **Favorite Retweet Reply**

**tmillerpoetry** natasha miller @YoungPhenom @jajapink if she chose to be a woman, who Am I to pick and choose when and where she should be treated like a man

15 Oct Favorite Reply Delete

155

**jajapink** @YoungPhenom @tmillerpoetry I was part of that debate too =p
15 Oct Favorite Reply

**Mic_Phelps** Microphone Phelps Judge Judy was a man lol
15 Oct Favorite Retweet Reply

**jajapink** @tmillerpoetry @YoungPhenom you know there are some men that like looking like a woman but still like women? If we were all good with this
15 Oct Favorite Reply

**jajapink** @tmillerpoetry @YoungPhenom no questions asked.... How could a person like myself be safe
15 Oct Favorite Reply

**Mic_Phelps** Microphone Phelps @jajapink @tmillerpoetry explain please

15 Oct Favorite Retweet Reply

**jajapink** @tmillerpoetry Why should I have to use restroom with a woman that was once a man... How do I know he's not looking at me... when I think
15 Oct Favorite Reply

**jajapink** @YoungPhenom @tmillerpoetry that i'm in a private place with women
15 Oct Favorite Reply

**Mic_Phelps** Microphone Phelps @jajapink @tmillerpoetry oh i get it.
15 Oct **Favorite Retweet Reply**

**tmillerpoetry** natasha miller @jajapink because sex change an sexual intentions have nothing to do with each other. I use the same restroom as women. I don't look at them
15 Oct Favorite Reply Delete

**tmillerpoetry** natasha miller @jajapink so if she's in the mens restroom and wants to be a woman she's probably looking at the men?
15 Oct Favorite Reply Delete

@jajapink and If she's in the womens restroom and use to be a man she's looking at the women?
15 Oct Favorite Reply Delete

**jajapink** @YoungPhenom what the men that still like women sexually even tho they like to look like women?
15 Oct Favorite Reply

**tmillerpoetry** natasha miller @jajapink @YoungPhenom wanting to have a sex change has nothing to do with wanting to be homosexual or heterosexual or sexual at all.
15 Oct Favorite Reply Delete

**Mic_Phelps** Microphone Phelps @jajapink Sex change, also called transsexuality, is a procedure by which an individual of one sex is
15 Oct **Favorite Retweet Reply**

**Mic_Phelps** Microphone Phelps

@jajapink hormonally and surgically altered to attain the characteristics of the other sex.
15 Oct Favorite Retweet Reply

**MissDanniLittle** @tmillerpoetry @youngphenom @jajapink beautiful debate love it!! I agree with T
15 Oct Favorite Undo Retweet Reply

**jajapink** @tmillerpoetry @jajapink @YoungPhenom I just think that you should stay the gender you were born. And if you want to change then cool
15 Oct Favorite Reply

**jajapink** Jaja Morgan @tmillerpoetry @YoungPhenom but there should be boundaries
15 Oct Favorite Reply

**Mic_Phelps** Microphone Phelps @tmillerpoetry @nochaserash but if ur of African descent n u change to white skin, ur white, but it doesn't change the fact ur African
15 Oct Favorite Retweet Reply

**Mic_Phelps** Microphone Phelps @tmillerpoetry @nochaserash so would you call them European if they changed their skin to white and changed their race on their birth certif
15 Oct Favorite Retweet Reply

**tmillerpoetry** natasha miller

@nochaserash if you bleach your skin the COLOR white you are the COLOR white if you change your skin to black you are the COLOR black.
15 Oct Favorite Reply Delete

158

**tmillerpoetry** natasha miller

@nochaserash however u are not identified as part of the African or Caucasian race bcus of a COLOR change. Race and gender changes are separate, no connection.
15 Oct Favorite Reply Delete

**Mic_Phelps** Microphone Phelps @tmillerpoetry @nochaserash u can't say that, because, ur born black, ur born a man, u change to white u change to a woman same shit lol
15 Oct Favorite Retweet Reply

**tmillerpoetry** natasha miller @YoungPhenom @nochaserash there is no procedure to change your race there is a procedure that takes place daily to change gender
15 Oct Favorite Reply Delete

**tmillerpoetry** natasha miller @YoungPhenom phenom shut up, because I'm sure you understand that the two are not the same AT ALL. Race is race, gender is gender.
15 Oct Favorite Reply Delete

**jajapink** @tmillerpoetry @jajapink @YoungPhenom question: If she goes to jail is she going to a womans prison?

**jajapink** RT @nochaserash @tmillerpoetry its like wanting to be white bleaching skin on the outside ur white but inside &genetically ur black
15 Oct Favorite Reply

**jajapink** @tmillerpoetry @nochaserash That's like saying when I wear weave my hair is long... It's not... The weave is long....

**tmillerpoetry** natasha miller @jajapink @nochaserash gender changes to weave? We're a lot more evolved in our thinking than this, I KNOW!
15 Oct Favorite Reply Delete

**Mic_Phelps** Microphone Phelps I can dress like a cat, remove my penis and get a vagina, whiskers,get fur on my skin, hang with cats, crawl like one. But IM NOT A CAT! lol
15 Oct Favorite Retweet Reply

**tmillerpoetry** natasha miller

@nochaserash having A PENIS or A VAGINA is not the only difference in becoming a woman or a man.
15 Oct Favorite Reply Delete

**Mic_Phelps** Microphone Phelps @tmillerpoetry @nochaserash but YOU think you're changing your SEX, ur still a MALE, u just choose to look like and be called a female
15 Oct Favorite Retweet Reply

**Mic_Phelps** Microphone Phelps @tmillerpoetry @nochaserash YOU CAN NOT REPRODUCE naturally
15 Oct Favorite Retweet Reply

**Mic_Phelps** Microphone Phelps @tmillerpoetry its the same CONCEPT. U can't say its not its OBVIOUSLY the same CONCEPT
15 Oct **Favorite Retweet Reply**

**Mic_Phelps** Microphone Phelps @tmillerpoetry @jajapink @nochaserash we're not comparing the importance T we're comparing the CONCEPT
15 Oct **Favorite Retweet Reply**

**tmillerpoetry** natasha miller @YoungPhenom if race and gender are the same they would be categorized as the same but they're not so they're not!
15 Oct Favorite Reply Delete

**tmillerpoetry** natasha miller @nochaserash the procedure is a lot more complicated that @YoungPhenom @jajapink wanna give it credit for. Research maybe?
15 Oct Favorite Reply Delete

**Mic_Phelps** Microphone Phelps @tmillerpoetry @jajapink @nochaserash you can never take it out of being personal. Ur personally tied to this. We're lookin at FACT
15 Oct **Favorite Retweet Reply**

**Mic_Phelps** Microphone Phelps @tmillerpoetry @jajapink @nochaserash Scientist and Doctors the people who research and perform these procedures will tell you.
15 Oct **Favorite Retweet Reply**

**Mic_Phelps** Microphone Phelps @tmillerpoetry @jajapink @nochaserash that yes the surgery makes them JUST LIKE a male or female, BUT genetically they are still man/gurl

161

**Mic_Phelps** Microphone Phelps **@tmillerpoetry @nochaserash** so what is the difference? If thats the case why do they (penis, vagina) have such an important part in the change?
15 Oct Favorite Retweet Reply

**tmillerpoetry** natasha miller @YoungPhenom they play important part because of the complicated procedure but it is not the only part, far from it.
15 Oct Favorite Reply Delete

**jajapink** @YoungPhenom @tmillerpoetry @jajapink @nochaserash not trying to be funny just using simple analogies in order to have an understanding
15 Oct Favorite Reply

**jajapink** @tmillerpoetry @YoungPhenom @nochaserash I'll credit but transgender's feelings and ideas are not the only ones that need to be considered
15 Oct Favorite Reply

**tmillerpoetry** natasha miller @jajapink I agree everyones feelings should be considered at all times but we as a whole can not let our feelings dictate rights
15 Oct Favorite Reply Delete

**Mic_Phelps** Microphone Phelps @tmillerpoetry they aren't both things used to describe who you are? At the start, can u choose ur race? can u choose ur gender? No
15 Oct Favorite Retweet Reply

162

**Mic_Phelps** Microphone Phelps @tmillerpoetry people get discriminated against because of race and because of gender.
15 Oct **Favorite Retweet Reply**

**Mic_Phelps** Microphone Phelps @tmillerpoetry your race is determined by your genetics, your sex is determined by your genetics. Sounds a lot alike to me
15 Oct **Favorite Retweet Reply**

**tmillerpoetry** natasha miller Not my prefRT @nochaserash: @tmillerpoetry just one question I've been watchin yall debate would u wanna date a girl that used to be a man
15 Oct Favorite Reply Delete

**tmillerpoetry** natasha miller

@nochaserash I've never been faced with the situation but I can't tell my heart what to do. I don't wanna date women without their
15 Oct Favorite Reply Delete

**tmillerpoetry** natasha miller

@nochaserash virginity or common sense or plenty of other things they've had but I do.
15 Oct Favorite Reply Delete

**tmillerpoetry** natasha miller

@nochaserash it's all about being in the know. Of course I would want to be told

163

but if I find out I would still be understanding.
15 Oct Favorite Reply Delete

**jajapink** @YoungPhenom @tmillerpoetry @nochaserash That's like when the transgender woman to man wanted to have a baby

YoungPhenom @tmillerpoetry @nochaserash the news said pregnant man and it was def a woman
15 Oct Favorite Reply

**tmillerpoetry** natasha miller @jajapink the news said pregnant man out of respect for the procedure bcus he is now a man
15 Oct Favorite Reply Delete

**tmillerpoetry** natasha miller Interesting considering he didRT @jajapink: I KNOw Right! RT @YoungPhenom @tmillerpoetry @jajapink BUT A MAN CAN"T HAVE A BABY!!!!! lol
15 Oct Favorite Reply Delete

**Mic_Phelps** Microphone Phelps I just noticed I don't really even give a fuck Im just bored. Because if Mike Jordan wanted to be an owl. whooooo am i to say sumthn. LMFAO
15 Oct Favorite Retweet Reply

**Mic_Phelps** Microphone Phelps And on top of all of that, I shouldn't be able to tell ur a transsexual anyway, and if I can u wasted ur money lol
15 Oct Favorite Retweet Reply

**jajapink** @YoungPhenom @tmillerpoetry @nochaserash but she stopped taking her hormones

15 Oct Favorite Reply

**jajapink** @YoungPhenom @tmillerpoetry @nochaserash she said she didnt have or organs taken out so that she could reserve the option to get pregnant
15 Oct Favorite Reply

**jajapink** @YoungPhenom @tmillerpoetry @nochaserash What type of shit is that
15 Oct Favorite Reply

**Mic_Phelps** Microphone Phelps @tmillerpoetry @jajapink you wanna be a man but you wanna have babies. So after he's done giving birth he's a man again?
15 Oct Favorite Retweet Reply

**Mic_Phelps** Microphone Phelps @tmillerpoetry @jajapink this aint about the other shit this about a girl getting a sex change to be a man. But still being a woman
15 Oct Favorite Retweet Reply

**Mic_Phelps** Microphone Phelps @tmillerpoetry @jajapink but oh wait I THOUGHT she was a MAN, but men don't have BABIES, cause they don't have a uterus but he does?
15 Oct Favorite Retweet Reply

**jajapink** @YoungPhenom @tmillerpoetry Seems convenient.. be what you want when it's Convenient

**jajapink** Youre right Rt @tmillerpoetry I agree everyones feelings should be

165

considered but we as a whole can not let our feelings dictate rights
15 Oct Favorite Reply

**tmillerpoetry** natasha miller Every system has flaws.

**Mic_Phelps** Microphone Phelps @tmillerpoetry @jajapink yea, but this is not a FLAW its making a choice. Why be called a man, if you keep all your female parts?
15 Oct Favorite Retweet Reply

**tmillerpoetry** natasha miller @YoungPhenom he didn't keep all of his female parts
15 Oct Favorite Reply Delete

**Mic_Phelps** Microphone Phelps @tmillerpoetry Two years ago Beatie decided to have a child, so he stopped his bimonthly hormone treatment and resumed menstruation
15 Oct Favorite Retweet Reply

**jajapink** @YoungPhenom @tmillerpoetry he wasnt a man at the point of carrying that child and not taking his hormones lol
15 Oct Favorite Reply

**tmillerpoetry** natasha miller @YoungPhenom he's a man while having that baby according to his sex change
15 Oct Favorite Reply Delete

**jajapink** @YoungPhenom @tmillerpoetry I <3 yall but I can't keep up any longer lol i'm too exhausted and i'm still at stinkin work #bah x-/
15 Oct Favorite Reply

**jajapink** Jaja Morgan I would rather have sex
15 Oct Favorite Reply

**tmillerpoetry** natasha miller @jajapink would rather be having sex @YoungPhenom doesn't care would argue about anything and millions of people around the world r dying
15 Oct Favorite Reply Delete

**tmillerpoetry** natasha miller @jajapink @YoungPhenom physically and emotionally because of the seriousness of these type of situations
15 Oct Favorite Reply Delete

**jajapink** Jaja Morgan @tmillerpoetry awww seriously? Stop it! you know better than that? I love all people and don't want anyone hurt. I most def care
15 Oct Favorite Reply

**Mic_Phelps** Microphone Phelps @tmillerpoetry You are Crazy
15 Oct **Favorite Retweet Reply**

**Mic_Phelps** Microphone Phelps @tmillerpoetry And to try to act like I'm sayn I don't care about ppl dying over this is idiotic. I just don't think she should play golf
15 Oct **Favorite Retweet Reply**

**tmillerpoetry** natasha miller

## New message

**To**    Enter a friend's name or email address

**Message**

CHAPTER7
What you do not understand, you should not, without proper
knowledge or certification, diagnose as sickness. I do not
understand all of the things that other people do, I do not
agree with all of the things that other people do but I do
understand that not understanding something does not make
that something less normal or sick. The doctors make the
diagnosis and they too are sometimes wrong.

**Send**   Cancel

http://youtu.be/KVtXnQ5_S34 *"You're just another faggot with a mental illness who needs to be shot. I hope you get a bullet in the back of your head when you and boyfriend are walking down the street holding hands you sick creature."*FagMurderer666 2 years ago

*This comment has received too many negative votes* hide
*"You might be used to hearing this, but YOUR A FAGGOT CARTERMAYES. You like to "remember" homosexual faggots? How bout you remember how this sick demented vile creature came to school everyday dressed like a transexual faggot and jacked off in the gym locker room jizzing all over the place as the boys were changing their clothes.. This animals deserved to die, and not just die the way he did.. he deserved to be tortured and mutilated and fucking burned at the stake for his sick disgusting acts"*
FagMurderer666 2 years ago

**Cartermayes Inbox**

**T.miller**

Faggot                                                                                              12/ 5/08
You honestly have to have no life, to sit on Youtube all day (judging by your mini feed) looking up homosexual videos and leaving hateful comments. I've been called a faggot plenty of times and nigger hell I'm use it. If Lawrence did these things then obviously he needed help, maybe prayer but not death. Look on the bright side though: you think all gay people are going to hell, and murders more than likely go to hell so once again you'll end up around the gay people you love to watch so much. See you around buddy cus I'm sure you'll be viewing and commenting on more gay videos. I pray for people like you!

FagMurderer666

**Re: faggot**                                     12/ 5/08
Nope I don't sit on youtube all day viewing gay videos, I'm on the internet less then 2 hours a day. It's so funny seeing you pathetic fucking faggots stick up for 1 another. Seeing a faggot defend his pride is quite honestly one of the funniest things I have seen. Two homosexual sick demented fuckers who find such an appeal in the same sex that they actually think there's nothing wrong with that, now that's just funny but at the same time sick and disgusting.
YOUR A FAGGOT!

 FagMurderer666

**Re: faggot** 12/ 5/08

God supports executions of faggots. He embraces us for preserving society and saving this world for eternal damnation from you filthy faggots and your homosexuality.

**Re: Re: faggot**

Yea I know because clearly being gay will end all of mankind. Two people of the same sex will just be the ending to the forever that we are all promised. Let me make this clear. I'm not defending SHIT to you, because I don't have to. I was myself when I woke up this morning and I'll b me when I go to bed at tonight. Your ignorance is nor a threat or a scare to me so if you think tough names like fagmurdered666 is frightening, you all fucking wrong. There's plenty of things that GOD don't support so when this world ends, I'm sure it'll be because we've all played our part.

 FagMurderer666

**Re: Re: faggot** 12/ 5/08

Maybe nobodies a threat to you on youtube right now but spread yourself around some more and profess your faggotry out in public and publicize that by holding hands with your homosexual lover and see if you don't get a bullet in the back of the head. It's happened many times,.

 **T.miller**

**Re: Re: Re: faggot** 12/ 5/08

I'm sure it has and just for you I'll go out with my lover everyday and hold hands. If I do get one to the back of the head, then hey that's' the price you pay for living. I just can't comprehend y u care so much. You're obviously not gay so do you: Get a woman, have kids, and save mankind! Although I'm sure it'll probably be hard to keep a woman once she realizes how sick you are. As I mentioned before, I pray for people like you and I will continue to do so. All of this other talk is irrelevant. I hope your sickness gets better and u find a cause to be for instead of one to be against.

 FagMurderer666

**Re: Re: Re: faggot** 12/ 5/08

The funny thing with all you sick demented faggots is you talk about mentall illnesses and cures but you don't realize your own fucked up mentall illnesses. The only problem is faggotry cannot be cured. Your scenario of straight people who hate faggots and saying that OTHER straight people will realize how sick we are is equivalent to a clinically insane patient trying to tell a SANE person that they are the insane one and that other sane people will realize it and have them committed

It might sound confusing, read it again and understand because it makes perfect sense.. You have no right to talk about mentall illness dumbass, because you suffer from one of the more serious mental disorders. Any dumbfuck that sees appeal in the same sex got some serious issues they need to resolve.

And don't speak for America or herosexuals because one thing this world doesnt want is faggots like you corrupting and polluting our economy.

 **T.miller**
**Re: Re: Re: Re: faggot**      12/ 5/08
So let me ask you this: if gay is a sickness or illness, wouldn't you be trying to help the people that suffer from it instead of killing them? Also let me say this, I have no problem with heterosexuality, I have problems with people that want to murder and hate people for doing things that they do not condone. We can talk about God and America and polluting the economy but sir, we would then have to talk about everything that takes part in that. I understand psychology well enough. I learned that when people have problems, you try to help and if you do not want to provide help you live and let live. See how we're writing back and forth because you think I have a problem and I think that you have a problem? The difference is, I'm very understanding towards your problem because with a name like fagmurderer666, which is a murderer and the devil you need some type of help. You can't talk about God sending people to hell but represent the devil because that obviously means you don't roll that tough with God. Now let me take a second to clear something else up. I am a woman so start calling me a lesbian instead of a fag although I know you'll probably say dyke cus u think it stings a lot more but it doesn't. This is very interesting tho so I hope you continue to write back but can u please be a little less aggressive?

 **T.miller**
**Re: Re: Re: Re: faggot**     12/ 5/08
P.S. I don't just stand up for the rights of gay people. I stand up for the human rights of all people.

Ahh, look at the foul mouthed ramblings of cowardly bigot boy. Nice person aren't you. cutedyke2 2 years ago 28

ANDYDIVA - So you'd beat up/kill a child. You're worthless, cowardly bigot boy. cutedyke2 2 years ago 31

Foul mouthed, cowardly scum. You can't SPELL and have very limited vocabulary.Get an education, preferably in Prison. You're a joke. mafiasdaughter 2 years ago 15

Oh, and you're a little cowardly piece of shit. You're not worthy of my time. Keep commenting and dishing out insults. I laugh at scum like you. Now get yourself some psychiatric help + some anger management. mafiasdaughter 2 years ago 12

Correction. It's scum like you who have no respect for anything. Oh, and learn proper English. Toss pot. mafiasdaughter 2 years ago 11

and you're an ignorant bigot. Someone who thinks a 15yr old boy should die because of his sexuality is a sociopath. Go and rot in hell. You are the dog shit on my shoe. mafiasdaughter 2 years ago 15

What sort of people say at 15yr old boy deserved to die? Just because he was psychiatric help. mafiasdaughter 2 years ago 13

174

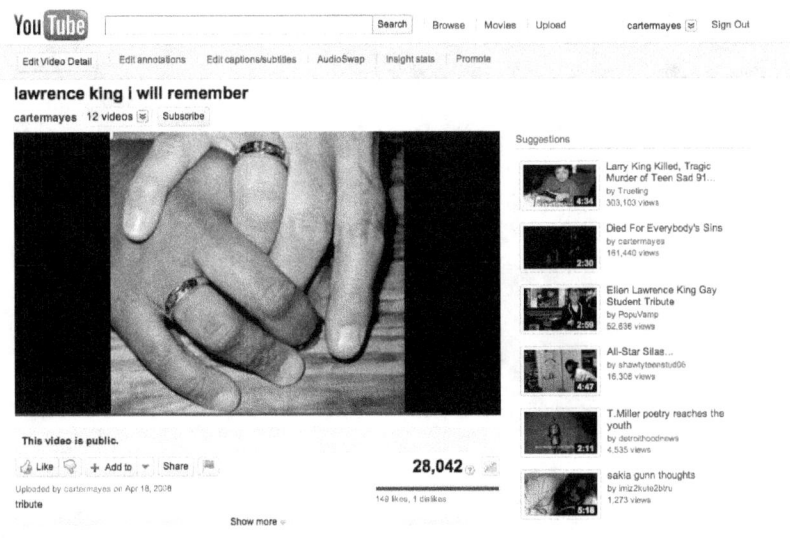
u r pathetic. Talking about someones death that way. 85beau 2 years ago

How can someone talk dwn on a child or those who are gay. Who makes you the upper power to say anything. I cry now in pain because there is no hope for us gay, and bis. But i stand on laughing at those who tend to hate. RIP to those.....xoxo tiffany78745 2 years ago 4

A 13-year-old who molests 3-year-olds is a pedophile! Do not try & tell me otherwise, JMasterHo95! SmooshedVaginaGal96 2 years ago

JMasterHo95, I know you are a gay pedo! I am sure that if you happened to be at a lil' boy's funeral & in the same room as his body with no one else there, you would: cut his dick off with a knife, put his dick into yer asshole scrotum first cuz you would love feeling the warm wet soft tissue where his dick was cut off touching yer anus as you stick it there, stick yer dick into the hole where you cut off his dick, & fuck him there while twirling his dick inside yer asshole, using it as a dildo! SmooshedVaginaGal96 2 years ago

thank you!!!!

we need people like you to stand up in this world. people to show whats going on in the world today my best friend almost killed himself cuz he was tired of people talking about who he is in how he lives his life in thank you cuz now were helping me in you are showing others to help in care!! queenkeke 2 years ago 3

He should have done it. Would have done society a favor. jwerner1469 2 years ago

175

## New message

**To** | Enter a friend's name or email address

**Message** | CHAPTER8
Matthew Wayne Shepard (December 1, 1976 – October 12, 1998) was tortured and murdered near Laramie, Wyoming.

Sakia Gunn (May 26, 1987 – May 11, 2003) was a 15-year old African American Lesbian who was murdered as a hate crime in Newark, New Jersey. Richard McCullough was charged with her death and sentenced to 20 years in prison

Jamey Rodemeyer (Mar 21, 1997– Sept 18, 2011) a 14-year-old boy from Williamsville, NY, took his life after years of bullying because his sexuality.

Lawrence "Larry" Fobes King (January 13, 1993 - February 13, 2008) was a 15-year-old openly gay student at E.O green junior high school in Oxnard, California. He was shot twice by fellow student, 14-year-old Brandon McInerney, and was kept on life support until he died two days later.

**Send**  **Cancel**

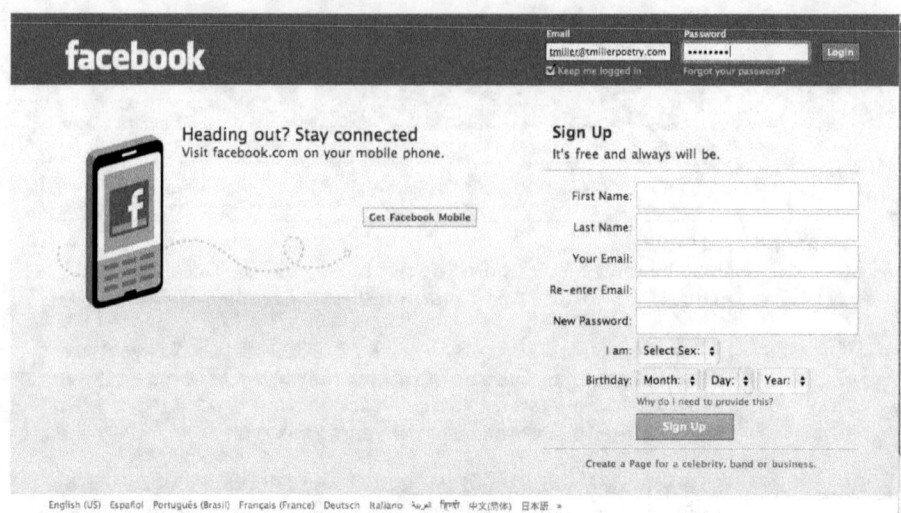

**ShowSum Courtesy'Curtis**
WHEN DID FAGGOTS START ROAMING THE EARTH S FREELY? SMH, I FEEL
ANOTHER HOLOCAUST COMING...LOL

July 3, 2010 at 3:25pm via Mobile Web · Like · Comment

 Stop talking about gay people!!
July 3, 2010 at 3:27pm · Like

 **ShowSum Courtesy'Curtis** SHUT UP QUEER!
July 3, 2010 at 3:29pm · Like

 lol
July 3, 2010 at 3:29pm · Like

 Lol!!
July 3, 2010 at 3:42pm · Like

 So u gon b tha first to b gased...lol
July 3, 2010 at 4:14pm · Like

 **ShowSum Courtesy'Curtis** lol... fuck you nigga, you prbly
hiding in the attic right now...They comin for yo ass
July 3, 2010 at 4:16pm · Like

 nigga, don't make me call a couple of my
queen homies to get in dat ass...I don't think u would want that
lol.
July 3, 2010 at 4:18pm · Like

 DLA!
July 3, 2010 at 4:19pm · Like

 **ShowSum Courtesy'Curtis** Lol @ Astrin...
July 3, 2010 at 4:21pm · Like

 Gays get on my nerves!
July 3, 2010 at 4:31pm · Like

Natasha's Profile · Natasha's Wall

**Natasha T. Miller**
Sept22nd Tyler Clementi an 18 -year- old student from Rutgers University jumped off a bridge and committed suicide after his roommate live streamed his sexual encounter with a man. A response from fellow student Lauren Felton:" had he been in bed with a woman this would not have happened. He wouldn't have been outed via an online broadcast and his privacy would've been respected and he might still have his life

October 1, 2010 at 4:55pm via iPhone · Unlike ·comment
5 others like this.

**Mila Willfords** i personally think that if it was two WOMEN having sex, it would have been GLORIFIED and MAXIMIZED.

and their feelings of love would have turned into a monetary gain, somethn like GIRLS GONE WILD or some other bullshit of that nature.

i think that this is fuckn RIDICULOUS.
i drive on BOTH sides of d street,
yet the LEFT side seems to have more traffic than the RIGHT :\

this is truly a sad Sad SAD situation...

may his soul live in splendid peace.
October 1, 2010 at 5:03pm · Like · 3 people

**Godschild** Thats so sad I heard abt it on Ellen... People get off on putting other people down! Lord rest his soul!
October 1, 2010 at 5:05pm · Like

**Nova Roswell** Yeah, I saw that yesterday..The roommate and another student are currently only being charged with a privacy felony...They should be charged with murder.
October 1, 2010 at 5:05pm · Like · 3 people

**Godschild** They need to be charged @nova!!! They got his blood on their hands!!! People make me sick!!!
October 1, 2010 at 5:09pm · Like · 3 people

**Nova Roswell** That was ridiculous. another boy in commited suicide because of his sexuality and badgering....smh
October 1, 2010 at 5:17pm via · Like

**Tara Mels** the roomate should be charged
October 1, 2010 at 5:39pm · Like

**Marie James** Wow.. Well obviously she is ignorant. No one should have their privacy ousted period! I don't care what their sexual orientation is. I feel bad though for people who can't be comfortable with who they are. I wish that he loved himself enough to know life is worth it and if u believe in what you do and who you are don't let anyone make u feel bad about it
October 1, 2010 at 5:51pm · Like · 2 people

**Natasha T. Miller** I just said there should be a grade school mandatory course on how to deal with humiliation. Shame can be so deadly.
October 1, 2010 at 5:55pm · Like · 3 people

**Dasia Loyd** HATERS SHOULD MIND THEIR OWN BUSINESS...NOW THEY HAVE TO LIVE WIT WAT THEY DID...MAY HE R.I.P
October 1, 2010 at 5:55pm · Like · 1 person

**Cass Renae** SMH was looking at that and u just wonder what was the frickin point of humiliating him?!? Its not just shame that's deadly, its ignorance, disrespect, misunderstanding and disregard for self or others!! I hope the charges and punishment is not light and that the family finds grounds to sue them too!! Not that it helps but maybe to bring attention and concern to the surface!!

October 1, 2010 at 6:27pm · Like · 1 person

**Rockie Amenson** Some people get pleasure outta others pain. It's down right sad that he did that and he should be charged with murder! I'm so sick of hate crimes. SMH! People should mind their own business!

October 1, 2010 at 6:33pm · Like

**Tiana combs Pretty** Teens are committing suicide at an alarming rate for more reasons than sexuality. I'm with T and marie, classes on how to deal with humiliation as well as courses on improving self-esteem should be mandatory in school. This is a sad case and my prayers are with the family of that child.

October 1, 2010 at 6:40pm · Like

**Daruis Genius Waleh** sad.

October 2, 2010 at 1:58am · Like

Write a comment...

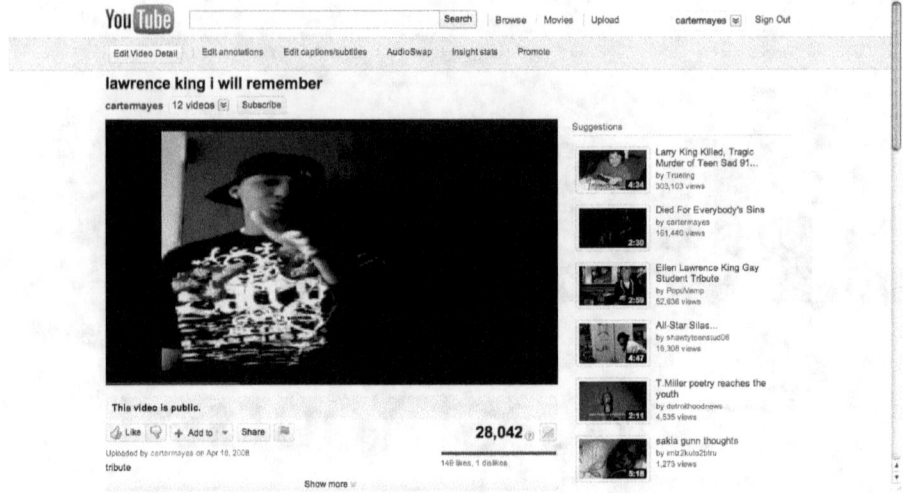

i loved it...im not gay but my mother, my cousin and some friends of mines are and I be so scared for them..*SO MANY TEARS* Munnings09 1 year ago

omg this touch me sooo much cause they killed one of my close frens the other day jus because she was gay..sigh.... we live in a cruel world.....u are an amazing poet!!!!! adjwoa90 1 year ago

You did a wonderful job. People shouldn't be killed just because they're different. Everyone is different in the world, I just don't understand why someone would kill someone else just for being different, GabrielEQ2009 1 year ago

lusti89, enjoy hell. you're just insecure ya jerk! deep poem. hit a lot of places. hatecrimes are ridiculous. everyone just needs to chill and have a good time and respect eachother for who we really are and not hate people for their labels or what they look like on the outside heyhaila09 1 year ago

.....well i personally dont like gays like wow what a lost soul.... but i wouldn't kill a gay. killerxzero 1 year ago

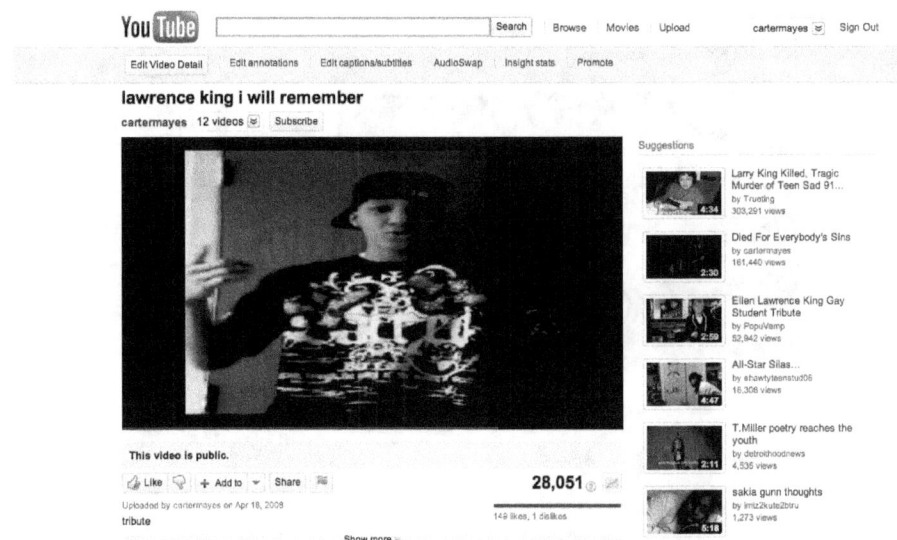

GAYS R HORRIBLE DISGUSTING &DESERV 2BURN ALIVE AS THEYRE
GONNA BURN IN HELL, THEYRE THIS & THAT. Blah blah f*ckin blah. it
amazes me dat homophobes think theyre sum how better than any LGBT ppl
while sayin the most hateful, sadistic, & disrespectful stuff u can imagine. its
pathetic &old already. sayin2 some1 u hate them cuz they r gay isnt gonna make
them change or adopt ur beliefs. Bottom Line a innocent boy was killed in his
prime. Yall r cruel for sayin he deserved it. Nice poem btw *snaps* DRArtist88 2
years ago

*This comment has received too many negative votes*   hide
Faggots don't deserve to live Footballpr27 2 years ago

*This has been flagged as spam*   hide
you dont deserve to live PaulSkinny 2 years ago


I love to have a man eat my ass am I normal? ava1onjoyous 2 years ago
2@ava1onjoyous **what a butt faggot** dukiedu 8 months ago

*This comment has received too many negative votes*   hide
oh fuck you and these videos. People are shot all the time for no reason so why
are you posting this 1 in a million time a homo was killed. Blacks are killed for
being black, whites are killed for being white, and hell kids are killed because
they cried too much and the step dad killed them. Shit happens. So fuck you and
this video. Spreading gayness on youtube is just fucked up. thedevirginizer27 2
years ago

185

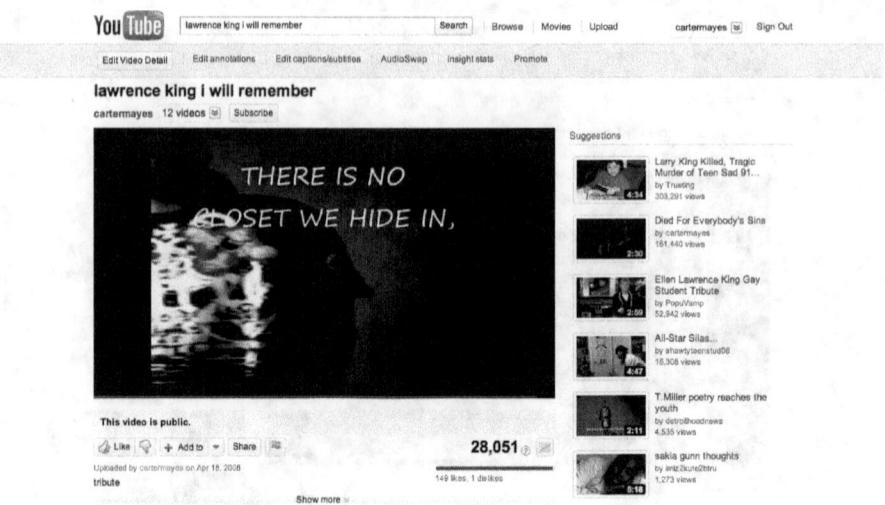

*This comment has received too many negative votes*  hide
No wonder your a fag. dragonlord10 2 years ago

If you're gonna use derogatory statements at least get it right! I'm not a fag! I'm dike you idiot! kerry31088 2 years ago

sad. nice video its sad how people could care so much for cruelty to animals [i love animals] or how someone can get marijuana to be legal but they dont make a scene for a child being killed for his sexual orientation.thats sad imBOMByea 2 years ago

como alguien puede defender a un asesino.. me pregunto si el q mato a este pibe .. hubiese tratado de ser invitado por una chica q no le gustaba .. o fea .. hubiese echo lo mismo? clara q es un crimen de odio !! leaneemo 2 years ago

if a gay did ever kill a straight person i would probarbly only be because they had been pushed too fat by the bullying and discrimination that person had put them through and not simply because of their sexuality gays know what it is like to be judged and are not likely to judge others based on their sexuzl preferences i mean for God sakes WHY does nit matter? very sad death and one that never had to happen he was so young he had his whole life ahead of him. RIP larry xxxxxxxx dclayden1 2 years ago

They say this was a "hate crime," and that may be true. It may not be, we may never find out. However, this brings a scenario to mind. Whenever a gay person is killed by someone who happens to be straight, it's automatically labelled "hate crime." If a straight person is murdered by someone who happens to be gay, we rarely (if ever) hear the term "hate crime." Why is that? If straight people kill gays because they're gays, don't gays have the ability to kill heteros for being straight?

kf8295 2 years ago

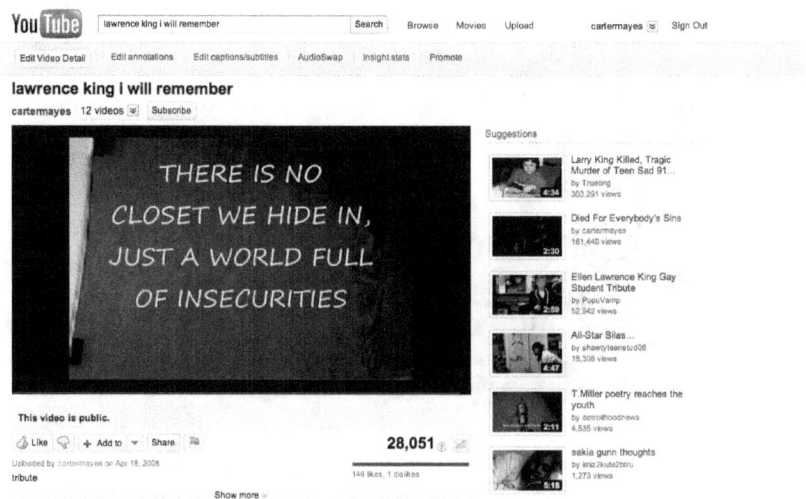

god bless you for speaking out. 24 year old gay male bashed a few times... survived... and this touched my heart.... if only someone could save all the innocent and hold them in their arms...if only...... takingovernyc 2 years ago

*This comment has received too many negative votes*   hide
WOW!! he got fucked In da ass Den Shot dat suckz lol OMGItzLTRE 3 years ago

You are the most ingnorant person to even think of gloating upon the tragedy of another regardless of your beliefs. That which you place on others will come back to you and much more worse. You're sick and inhumane, you bastard, probably conceived out of incest..!! sassybutclassy79 3 years ago

That was beautiful. its sad to see the kind of world we live in where we are treated like shit and murdered just because we are open about who we love. Its Just So Sad. R.I.P. Lawrence King jhajha05 3 years ago 2

You are amazing. Thank you so much for standing up for us! LGBTQ people need to stand together more often. datgurl49 3 years ago 2

wow ...thtz so sad..i remember when lil dude died ...ya wordz were right...I got mad tearz rollin mequa102 3 years ago

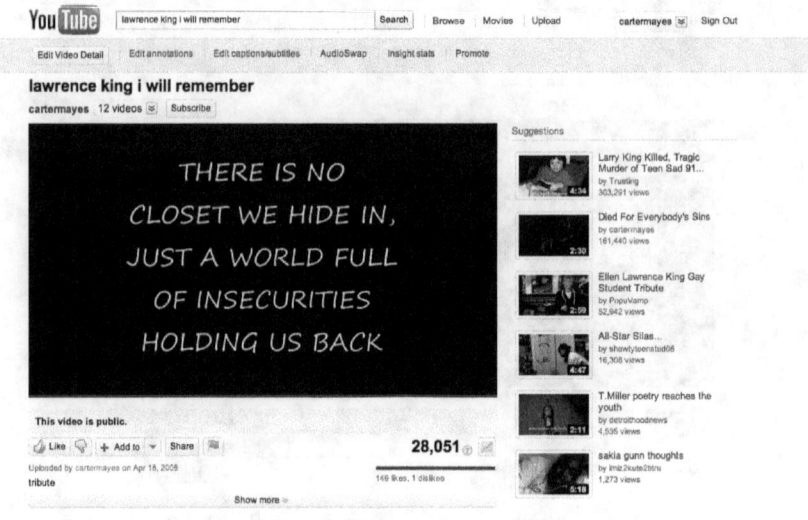

*This comment has received too many negative votes*   hide
**one less queer to deal with** drumigniter 3 years ago

www.ingramcontent.com/pod-product-compliance
Lightning Source LLC
Chambersburg PA
CBHW060257290526
45789CB00001B/343